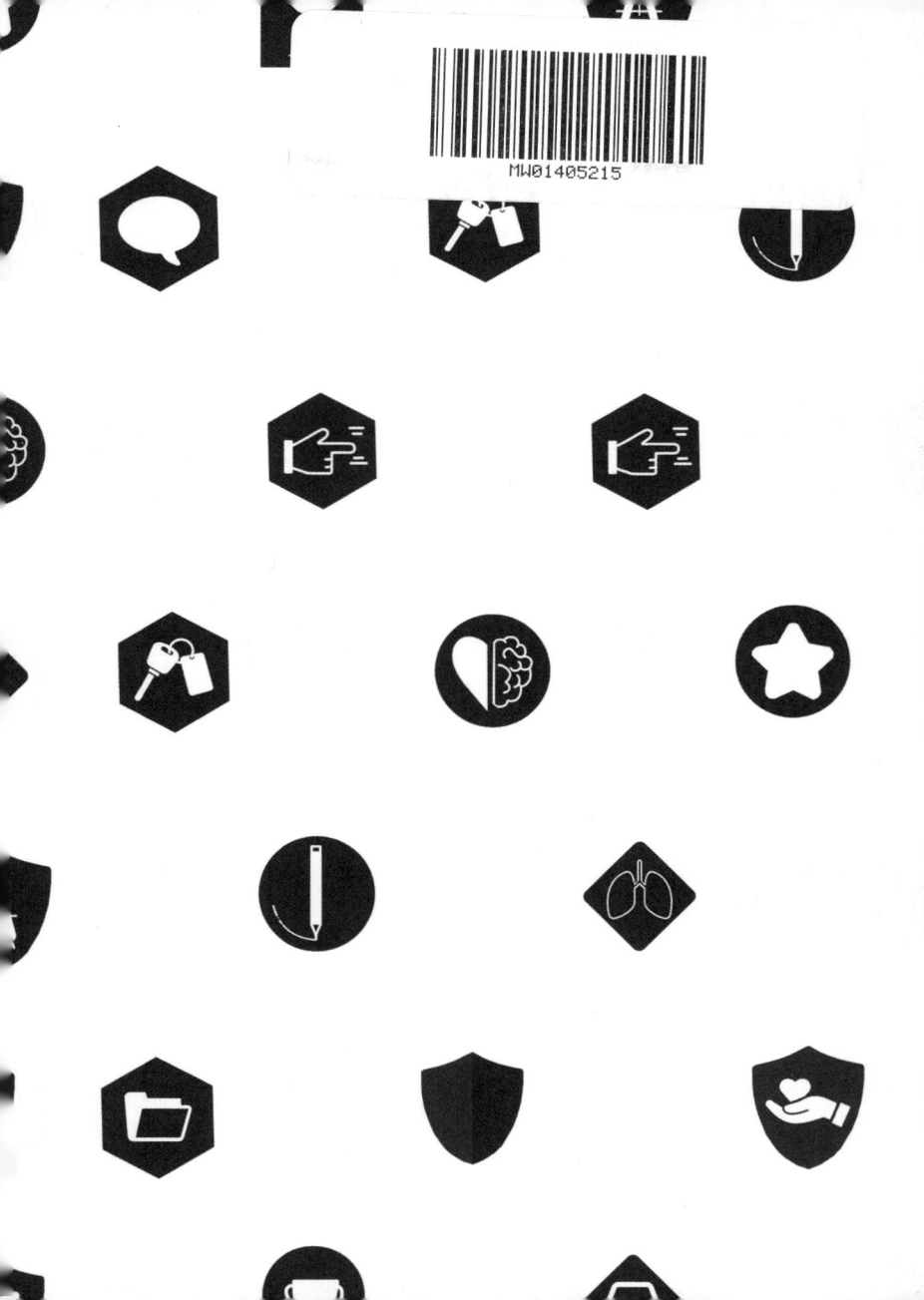

AM I DOING THIS RIGHT?

Making Choices without Mom Guilt

Text copyright © 2025 by Rebecca Fox Starr
Illustration copyright © 2025 by Mckay Rappleyea
All rights reserved.

Published by Familius LLC, www.familius.com
PO Box 1249, Reedley, CA 93654

Familius books are available at special discounts for bulk purchases, whether for sales promotions or for family or corporate use. For more information, contact Familius Sales at orders@familius.com.

Reproduction of this book in any manner, in whole or in part, without written permission of the publisher is prohibited.

Library of Congress Control Number: 2024948384

Print ISBN 9781641704465
EBook ISBN 9798893960433

Printed in China
Edited by Michele Robbins and Peg Sandkam
Cover and book design by Mckay Rappleyea

10 9 8 7 6 5 4 3 2 1

First Edition

AM I DOING THIS RIGHT?

Making Choices without Mom Guilt

Rebecca Fox Starr, LMSW

CHOOSE YOUR MOTHERHOOD ADVENTURE

This book is dedicated to three of the finest parents I know: Mom, Dad, and Emily, who have always encouraged me to choose my own adventure while showing me that a person can be resilient, brave, tender, tough, wise, humble, curious, and kind—all at once. It is because of you that I am here today.

Preface 7

Introduction 10

Part 1 The Baby Stories 13

    Chapter 1 Your Trench is the Finest Trench:
A Mindfulness Story
    Bonus: Your Middle-of-the-Night Companion
    Chapter 2 They Call Me the Baby Whisperer:
A Boundaries Story
    Bonus: Set Your Boundaries
    Chapter 3 Smiling While You Are Simply
Surviving: A Communication Story
    Bonus: Pop Your Negative Thought Bubbles

Part 2 The Kid Stories 61

    Chapter 4 Tired in Your Bones:
A Planning-Ahead Story
    Bonus: Prep Your Own Pep Talk
    Chapter 5 Blackbeard is Mushy Food Intolerant:
A Judgment Story
    Bonus: Make the Perfect Plate
    Chapter 6 Romanticizing the Mundane:
A Support Story
    Bonus: Be Your Own BMFF

Part 3 The Tween/Teen Stories 107

    Chapter 7 I Can't Stop it From Raining, but I
Can Give You an Umbrella: A Self-Respect Story

Bonus: Create Your Tween/Teen Survival Kit
Chapter 8 Your Carbon Footprint!?: A Wise Mind Story
Bonus: Mind Your Wise Mind
Chapter 9 Flattering and Shattering: A Rupture and Repair Story
Bonus: Create a More/Less Inventory

Badge Index and Celebratory Sash Ceremony   155

Notes and Further Reading   161

Preface

Dear Reader,

I had been working on this book for almost a year and had been wading through the pandemic for nearly two, when I had an epiphany. Well, an epiphany and COVID.

These facts are not entirely unrelated.

I was lying on the couch, coughing, aching, ailing, as the rest of my family members were also recovering from the virus, when I was walloped by an overwhelming emotion: guilt. I was feeling terribly guilty about the fact that my kids, at almost twelve and eight at the time, both with symptomatic COVID, both in quarantine, had been spending too much time on their screens, and wondered if I should have been doing more to entertain them. The question plagued me, spinning like a carousel in my mind:

"Am I doing this right?"

As sick as I felt, I still had room for those less-than lies and was *shoulding* all over myself. Those unrelenting thoughts convinced me I was doing less than I could. The notion that I should be doing more for my kids as far as education, stimulation, activity, exercise, and fun; that my skills were less than ideal and I *should* be handling things with more grace; and that in small, yet consistent ways, I was failing was ever-present.

In that moment, when the absurdity of the situation hit me, it clicked. I had been overlooking another affliction, one that was also plaguing people I knew and loved, and one for which there has been no known cure or vaccine: *parent guilt,* with all its weight and endlessly shapeshifting permutations, as well as the ability to take away all confidence and perspective in one fell swoop.

If a friend—or, really, anyone—ever expresses these feelings of parent guilt to me, I reassure them that they are awesome and they have nothing to feel guilty about. I truly believe all parents are awesome and they have nothing to feel guilty about. I'd make sure to tell them that they *are* doing this right. If a friend were sick and expressed feelings of guilt about not doing enough special activities with their kids (who also happened to be sick) I would find it preposterous.

Why is it so much easier to be kind to others, and so much more challenging to have compassion for ourselves?

The fact that I had this epiphany while sick with COVID is irrelevant, as it could have been any illness from any source at any time. I went into the 2020 pandemic as an anxious person and used much of my time in the subsequent years to heal. I found calm and contentment when I learned to accept that which I could not control and, even more importantly, that which I would not want to control. I made up my mind to tackle my own case of parent guilt just as I was facing the virus: with patience, fortitude, tenacity, and the right tools.

I used self-talk, mindfulness, and many of the techniques I had learned throughout the years. I studied and built muscles that I did not know existed, muscles that look like boundaries and self-care and dialectical thinking. In 2022, I decided to fortify my clinical expertise and went back to school for my master's in social work and have since become a Licensed Master of Social Work, or LMSW. I learned how to help myself and wanted to translate my experience into helping others. I studied the works of psychological experts like Dr. Aaron Beck, the founder of Cognitive Behavioral Therapy, and Dr. Marsha Linehan, who created Dialectical Behavioral Therapy (more on those concepts in a bit). Like many subjects, we can learn these skills on an academic level and then work to use the skills on a practical level. And just like anything else, these things take practice. If I can do it, anyone can do it, and so I wanted to make these tools accessible for everyone. I learned that the more you use these coping mechanisms, the more adept you will become. The more you're able to flex these muscles in times of calm, the easier it is to access them in times of distress.

I know how it feels to work tirelessly to be the best parent I can be while simultaneously always wanting to do better. I have a feeling you do too. The more you give yourself grace, the more your children learn to do the same for themselves. Giving yourself grace is giving permission and emphasis around the importance of self-compassion; it is modeling the possibilities of growth and how to make mistakes and, with resilience, keep going. What a gift that is for your children and, importantly, for you.

I've taken the lessons tools from my battles with parent guilt combined with my clinical experience in being a therapist and share them with you in a unique format: a choose your adventure for parents. I hope that this book is both helpful and entertaining. At the very least, please know you're not alone. You're not alone in your struggling, and you're not alone in your shoulding or less-than lies or moments of doubt that feel so true they can almost take you down with their enormity.

As we tackle all the things that ail us, we become a stronger force. With abundant gratitude and hope for brighter days,

Becca

Introduction

  Welcome to your story! Within these pages, you will choose your own path(s), much like the choose your own adventure books you may have read as a kid. Those stories were fun, exciting ways to take risks by relying on your instincts. You trusted your intuition to brave unknown paths! Yet, with age, that trust in our own intuition can become harder to access. If you are like many parents, you likely ask yourself, "Am I doing this right?". We all get bogged down with self-doubt, perpetual worry, and mom-guilt. This doubt, worry, and guilt erode our belief in ourselves. But fear not! In this book, you'll rediscover the power of trusting your instincts and charting your course with confidence. You'll learn that there is no single, right way.

  Keep in mind this is *your* story. There is no right or wrong; there is not even one, singular path. You will experience stories of parenting every stage of childhood with topics surrounding sleep, eating, boundaries, and compassion as these are experiences that are universal. The details are just for fun. Keep in mind that the stories about babies or children or teens, as well as the coping mechanisms you learn in each section, will likely apply to children of all ages. These are just a few examples in the endless sea of possibilities. There is no choice that is better than another, and with each option, you'll learn more about yourself and gain tools for your metaphorical toolbelt.

  These tools are a fusion of evidence-based interventions and insights gained from lived experiences. They are informed by treatments including Cognitive Behavioral Therapy (CBT) and Dialectical Behavior Therapy (DBT), offering practical assistance in navigating your parenting journey with confidence and resilience. CBT techniques focus on identifying and challenging negative thought patterns, while DBT skills emphasize mindfulness, emotional regulation, interpersonal effectiveness, and distress tolerance. Together, these tools can help you stay present and make decisions that align with your values and goals.

To remind you of this, you'll be collecting badges (known as *coping mechanisms*). You will also find activities, graphics, and visual aids just to give you a little boost along the way.

You will learn to become comfortable with your choices, even when they feel hard. Why? Because you deserve it.

Feel free to explore different paths, revisiting this book as often as you please. Each read-through offers fresh opportunities to forge new trails and embark upon unique experiences.

Let's do this. Let the adventure begin!

If you are:

A PARENT, turn to page 13.

SOMEONE WHO KNOWS A PARENT, turn to page 153.

Hi, Parent! If you are the parent of a . . .

BABY, turn to page 14.

KID, turn to page 61.

TWEEN/TEEN, turn to page 107.

The Baby Stories

In which we discuss:
Mindfulness
Boundaries
Communication

Chapter 1: Your Trench is the Finest Trench

A Mindfulness Story

Once upon a time, in a land very, very, very far away, there lived a beautiful maiden who had a wonderful life, perfect hair, a great job, meaningful friendships, a thriving marriage, and a preternaturally well-behaved baby. When she became a parent—specifically, as soon as she became a parent—she and her baby fell into a blissful, dependable, inexorable routine during which her baby ate well, played well, and slept well with the innate ability to fall asleep with just a gentle kiss on the forehead.

Knowing the baby would rest peacefully for a couple of hours, this maiden could treat herself to a daily nap. She knew the

importance of sleep for her overall mental and physical health, and, truthfully, had nothing better to do. When you're so efficient with your tasks—*as she was*—and have abundant help—*which she did*—a daily nap ritual makes perfect sense. Also, her hair would never get messed up from a little nap, obviously. She and the baby would awake from their nap simultaneously, ready to take on the rest of their enchanted, enchant*ing* day.

This maiden, joyful and lovely, is, ironically, the reason for so much dismay: the reason why people have been repeating the faulty, often unrealistic pieces of advice, like telling a parent to sleep while the baby sleeps. Because sleeping on command isn't possible. Because this maiden doesn't exist. She is a figment of our imagination serving to make other parents *real parents*, feel bad about themselves, their jobs, their marriages, their routines, their bodies, and, obviously, their hair.

You've heard this story. In fact, it's been repeated to you! And it's always coupled with the message that even if you find this time hard, you should be, at the very least, okay.

It is extremely hard to feel okay about doing the exact opposite of what you're told you should be doing.

You *should* be feeling happy, grateful, hopeful, blissful, full of only positives, because you are a parent and how could anything having to do with a parent or a baby not be beautiful?

Except this story is not only unrealistic, it is irresponsible, in that it sets up a completely unrealistic expectation. As a result, real parents, those who are not in a land far away, but rather here, in this land, in the trenches, are made to feel they are failing at everything, including their own self-care.

This "perfect mom" story has become a part of your muscle memory. Her image shows up at the most inconvenient of times: when you are feeling weepy, or when you accidentally smear poop on your face, or, in this case, when you are just trying to get a couple hours of rest.

Just as the maiden in the story is about to use her baby's tummy-time to do a tutorial on "how to achieve the perfect beach waves without using heat" . . .

You begin to wrestle with consciousness.

You open your eyes, searching for the sun in the darkness. You check the clock on your phone, even though you're not supposed to look at blue light; it's not good sleep hygiene.

The digital clock on your phone blares with a most offensive time: 2:56 a.m..

It is illuminated in white, in front of the image of your new baby, who, in the photo, is flashing a gummy smile and just being the absolute cutest.

As you shake the dreams from your head, and before your brain can make any rational connections, you hear a kind of melody, a soft cacophony.

It's your new normal, so many quiet sounds, all at once. The sounds of the room have been clashing against the sounds of your slumber, the soundtrack of your dreams. You hear white noise coming from an app on your phone, the whoosh of the fan as it whirs overhead, and the sounds of a not-quite-awake-but-not-quite-sleeping baby from over the monitor. Your partner, next to you, makes a rattling sound with each breath.

If this is the new symphony, you're its new conductor. You're familiar with the structure of the different notes as they come together at once. You're just not sure if you're, mentally or physically, ready to take the stage.

When the baby stirs like this it's a gentle warning. An overture, of sorts. She could be waking soon, which would mean that one of you would have to get up with her. But then again, the baby *could* soothe herself.

You have a choice: do you preemptively wake your partner, instructing them to give the baby a bottle, knowing that the baby may or may not wake up, you may or may not be able to go back to sleep, and they may or may not be grouchy in the morning. Your charged thoughts are coming in staccato and played in minor chords. They are notes that, in one way or another, sound wrong.

You are not the fair maiden. You are not the "perfect mom" or partner or conductor. But you are certainly trying to be the best parent you can be.

Your trench is the finest trench; the one that was made just for your family. It fits them beautifully. You just struggle to convince yourself of that. You wish this were easier and hold onto the words your more-seasoned parent friends have said to you over the last few weeks, assuring you that you *will* sleep again. It's hard to believe, but you simply have to have faith (or so they say).

You are faced with a choice. Choices are hard to make in the best of circumstances, let alone while in a state of perma-exhaustion.

CHOICE POINT: DO YOU WANT TO GET UP OR GO BACK TO SLEEP?

CHOICE 1: If you choose to get up, turn to page 18.
CHOICE 2: If you choose to go back to sleep, turn to page 27.

CHOICE 1: You've chosen to get up.

You rub your eyes, swing your legs over the side of your bed, and creep into the next room, where your baby is stirring. The pediatrician has assured you that these middle-of-the-night feedings are normal for such young babies, and that those parents who claim that their babies "have slept through the night since day one!" are the exception, not the rule.

"Yeah, or liars," you smirk to yourself as you assume the feeding position.

But, it's hard not to compare yourself. You constantly question what you could be doing differently as a new parent. What could you be doing better to make things easier for yourself and happier for your baby. It is not that either of you are unhappy; it's just so much more draining than you'd imagined, which

leads you to sometimes, in these lonely moments, wonder if you're simply doing it wrong.

Competition is tough, but mom-petition, the comparison between you as a parent and all of the parents you hear about/look up to/see/know, can feel crushing. You signed up to be a parent, but not for this fierce level of mom-petition.

You pick up your baby and nuzzle her, inhaling what she's exhaled. Her breath is somehow sweet, and you savor these fleeting exchanges. It's weird and, also, makes total sense.

You settle in to the seat on your rocker, a soft, cushiony chair that is hideous and luscious.

"Is this what they mean when they talk about #selfcare or instruct you to 'treat yo'self' in all the social media posts and on the parent group pages?"

You think of the maiden in your dream, with her perfect beach waves, and decide that her couch would be equally comfortable, but also the chicest. Though, she'd never be up during the night. Heaven forbid!

As though it's an instrument you've been practicing but not yet mastered, you begin the baby's feeding.

SUB-CHOICE POINT: How would you like to feed the baby?

SUB-CHOICE 1: If you decide to breastfeed the baby, turn to page 20.

SUB-CHOICE 2: If you decide to give the baby a bottle, turn to page 22.

SUB-CHOICE 1: Breastfeeding the baby

It is amazing how something so "natural" can feel so strange, not just for your body, but also mentally. Existentially. You've been breastfeeding consistently, and have certainly gotten the hang of it (the football hold and side-lying positions work best for you), but that doesn't make it any less difficult. Demanding. Draining. Even, at times, demoralizing.

Your breasts ache as you give yourself a mental reminder to get some more nipple ointment. For a human with no teeth, your baby most certainly leaves a mark.

You had always wanted to breastfeed, and so you feel grateful that you've been able to do so while also providing your little girl with the nourishment she needs. However, you'd be lying if you said it wasn't a million times harder than you could have imagined.

You've wrestled with supply issues, clogged ducts, and one particularly brutal case of mastitis. Despite the challenges, it's going well. Still, you're not sure how much longer you can keep up with exclusively nursing. It is just so hard.

But, it's equally hard to think of giving it up, both for reasons that are selfish and unselfish. As to the former, you don't like to fail at things. Yes, you'd have had breastfeeding success, and yes, you'd have given it a valiant effort, but you'd always planned to breastfeed for one year. You don't like to overpromise and underdeliver. As to the latter, you would feel terrible depriving your baby of the most perfect form of nourishment, created by your own body for their own body. You'd hate to think of sacrificing that for your own comfort.

Ultimately, from somewhere deep within you, you really do know that you've done an admirable job, as you've fed your baby the food she needs, and you know that you're lucky to have been able to experience breastfeeding at all, and you know that this decision will weigh on you no matter what, and you know that you have exactly zero energy at the moment to reconcile all of these things you think you know but don't know if you know or not.

For now, you just have to feed the baby. Your breasts are starting to ache and her little mouth is rooting. Fed is best.

Turn to page 24 to return to the story.

SUB-CHOICE 2: Bottle-feeding the baby

You shake your baby's bottle, feeling grateful that you've been able to provide her with the nourishment she needs. But, along with that gratitude, you feel the familiar pang. The wistful wondering of what could have been.

You'd considered breastfeeding, and even tried it for a couple of weeks, but you'd come to the conclusion that it was not the best option for you. Well, you and the baby's pediatrician had come to this conclusion, as your supply just wasn't robust enough to meet the baby's needs. You'd felt like a failure, which was particularly crushing in those first days. You remember sitting in your car after that doctor's visit and sobbing. It's not that you'd been dead set on breastfeeding, or that you even liked doing it, as you certainly did not, but it was taken from you. Not only did you have to contend with postpartum hormones, you had to wrestle with the hormones from weaning, and it had been really, really rough. You envied those people who had no interest in breastfeeding from the start, and felt completely content with giving their babies bottles from day one. That just wasn't you.

But you got through it, and you switched your baby to formula. Though many people claim that bottle-feeding would provide you with more freedom, you'd be lying if you said it wasn't a million times harder than you could have imagined. You're constantly plagued by guilt about your decision, even though this new style of feeding is going well and the baby is growing perfectly.

It's just that every time someone leans over your shoulder, admiring your sweet baby, and asks, "Oh, are you nursing?"

you feel like you've failed in some small, or, depending on the circumstance, not-so-small, way.

New parenthood is just so hard. You know that you've done an admirable job, as you've fed your baby, and that is just what the baby needs, and you know that you're lucky to have the security to do so, and you know that this decision would weigh on you no matter what, and you know that you have exactly zero energy at the moment to reconcile all of these things you think you know but don't know if you know or not.

For now, you just have to give the baby a bottle. Fed is best.

Turn to page 24 to return to the story.

One other surprising fact about new parenthood is that, along with being enchanting and magical, it can be extremely draining, lonely and, even, boring.

While it might feel virtuous to use this time to listen to informative podcasts or to read a classic piece of literature you've been meaning to get around to, you turn, as always, to your phone. It's amazing what a lifeline that little thing has become.

In the middle of the night, when things feel really dark, it has become your companion, your pediatrician, your friend. You know better than to trust everything you read, but it's helpful to distract yourself. It makes you feel less alone. When the rest of the world is asleep, you have camaraderie at your fingertips.

You feel guilty about wasting your time as there is so much more you could be doing during the time you're spending on Instagram. You could be updating the family calendar! Catching up on emails! Shopping for baby supplies, or groceries, or the birthday present for your cousin that you keep telling her is in the mail! It seems everyone has unrealistic expectations about what a new parent should be capable of juggling!!!

Your mind pivots to the list of real chores that awaits you. The laundry to do! The returns to make! The piles and piles and piles of things that drive you crazy while simultaneously feel impossible to tackle! Guilt weighs on you like it's a real, palpable thing you are holding along with your baby.

You're lost in your thoughts when you hear your baby make a soft, sweet, coo.

"I'll never get tired of listening to those sounds," you say to yourself.

You try to mentally conjure your favorite new-baby sounds, while simultaneously struggling to keep your eyes open.

They feel as though they're weighed down with sandbags. That feeling has become all too familiar as of late.

You need to stay awake but don't want to ruminate on all of your to-do items, as you simply don't have the energy. And that's when you remember: The 5-4-3-2-1 grounding exercise.

Grounding yourself has been a helpful tool, as it always serves to calm you while also keeping you focused. When thoughts swirl, grounding yourself helps to slow the tempo of things. It's easier to handle anything and everything after settling yourself in these moments.

You repeat the instructions that you've practiced to yourself:

> 5-4-3-2-1.
> You remind yourself to name:
> 5 things you can see.
> 4 things you can touch.
> 3 things you can hear.
> 2 things you can smell.
> 1 thing you can taste.

You look around the dim nursery and see a music box, a bottle of diaper cream, a bird suspended from a mobile, a folder from the pediatrician, and the stuffed dog you bought when you first found out you were pregnant.

You touch the fuzz on top of the baby's head, the ugly oh-so-cozy pillow supporting your back, the fleece of the baby's sleep sack, and the weight of the bottle and baby in your two arms.

You hear the whooshing of the sound machine, the adorable sucking sound of your baby drinking, and a plane on an overnight haul flying overhead.

You smell lavender and deliciousness: your baby's signature scent.

You taste the sweet satisfaction of flexing your mindfulness muscle. You're doing it. You're trying, in this moment, to be the best you for yourself and everyone around you. So, you taste that. . . well, that, and strawberry ChapStick.

You place your now dreamy baby back into the crib. You're up, and, though you're still positively wiped, not sure if you'll be able to fall back to sleep, you assure yourself that it will be okay either way. The worry feels less alive now. You know it intellectually, but it doesn't rule you.

And that, you can handle. As you tiptoe back into your bedroom, the sounds of your own quiet orchestra greet you once more.

Congratulations! You've Collected Coping Mechanism Badge of *Sensory Grounding*.

Turn to page 30 to return to the story.

CHOICE 2: You've chosen to go back to sleep.

You pull the covers over your head, desperate not to miss this precious window.

You know that worrying about getting back to sleep will only have the opposite of the intended effect and you'll rile yourself up, albeit unintentionally, but it's hard not to fret about squandering your opportunity.

Everyone talks about sleep these days.

"How are you sleeping?"

"How is the baby sleeping?"

"You know that sleep is so important!"

It's endlessly hard that something that is so important also feels so stressful.

You feel beat—you are beat—and yet you still manage to momentarily beat yourself up about not being perkier, not being the one to feed the baby, and for not being there to meet the needs of your child or your partner. You are tempted to calculate how many hours of sleep you'd get if you just fell asleep within however many minutes. But, you try not to.

"This is just one part of one night," you remind yourself, trying to do the thing you're supposed to do, involving stepping back from things so that you can put those things into perspective. You've learned that taking the pressure off of things, especially in that vulnerable state, gives you the best results.

"Honey?" you nudge your partner, gently enough to be respectful, but firmly enough to get your point across.

You are immediately regretful, second-guessing your choice to try to get more rest. You waffle back and forth so vigorously that you are like one of those giant, flailing creatures waving their graceless bodies outside of car-washes.

"You can still get up now," you tell yourself.

"I can still get up now," you then tell your partner.

You don't mean to be passive-aggressive, but it's hard to ask for things. Even when you know they would be okay with it. Perhaps, because you know they will be okay with it. You wish you could just clearly and directly ask them to take this shift, sharing just how tired you are feeling in this very moment, but, for now, you're picking the battles you forge with yourself. Because, again, you're just so tired.

"No, it's fine, go back to bed," they grumble at you, either very sleepy or moderately grumpy or both. You don't probe. See: extreme exhaustion.

As you settle back into your preferred sleep position (which is, obviously, on your right side, with your right arm under the pillow, your left knee crossed over your torso, and your left hand up against your face, in a position that calms you) you try your best to settle yourself.

You'd always expected to be the one to greet the baby during these sacred, middle-of-the-night feedings. You'd expected to add this to your growing list of rituals. You'd expected to be able to survive on little sleep, little alone-time, little self care, but, alas, you're just so relentlessly human.

You love being a parent with every ounce of your being and you feel like it's the hardest thing you've ever done, bar none, without question. So much of it is confusing, nerve wracking, new, and, dare you say it, boring. You constantly feel lonely, though you're never ever alone.

Parenthood is more magical than you could have imagined, and you love your baby fiercely and eternally. It's just a tremendous amount of emotion to be coursing through your still-healing body, all at once, all day, every day.

29

You need many things but, in this moment, you need nothing more than sleep.

You lean on your favorite mindfulness exercise: the practice of square breathing.

As you focus on your breath, breathing so deliberately, your mind and body will be coaxed into relaxation.

So, you begin.

You imagine yourself painting a square with your breath, allowing for four seconds to mentally paint each side.

You breathe in for four seconds, picturing yourself creating one side of the square.

You hold your breath for four seconds, while you craft the second side. You breathe out for four seconds, as the third side is created.

You hold your breath for the last four seconds as your square is completed.

You repeat your deep, intentional breathing until you start to lose count, your mind flitting between your consciousness and your dreams.

Your thoughts undulate as you fall peacefully into a new dream. You've done it. The hard thing. And now, it's time for rest.

Congratulations! You've Collected Coping Mechanism Badge of *Square Breathing*.

Turn to page 30 to return to the story.

BONUS: Your Middle-of-the-Night Companion Activity Guide

Hi, you! It's me, here: your bearer of connection and distraction, for when you need it most. Lonely? Bored? Overwhelmed?

I've got you, mama! Let me keep you company. Remember, you're not alone. Even when it feels like this. The way you feel right now is normal, temporary, and just another example of a hard thing you can do. So, let's do this.

IMPORTANT Grocery List

Except, it's not. Now that I've got your attention—because I KNEW you'd look at the grocery list page because you are, well, you—I present you with a different kind of list: a list of ten things you've done today. I do not mean "accomplishments" but, rather, things you've done. For example:

1. I opened my eyes.
2. I put toothpaste on my toothbrush.
3. I yawned.

See what I mean? I want you to make this list, making sure to honor the innocuous and mundane. How many items can you come up with?

_____

_____

_____

_____

_____

Look at you! You did it! EXCELLENT JOB! KEEP IT UP! OR NOT! YOU'RE THE BEST!

Haiku (How Are You?)

Hey, parent, hey! Have you written a haiku yet today? Oh? You haven't! Well, what are you waiting for?

As I'm sure you know, a haiku is a Japanese poem of seventeen syllables, in three lines of five, seven, and five, traditionally evoking images of the natural world. For example:

>I am a parent
>Even when I don't feel good
>I am always good.

Here, it's your turn! For the first one I'm happy to hold your hand:

>I am _____ (add three syllables)
>Even when _____ (add four syllables)
>I am always _____ (add one more syllable)

Your turn!

Well, that was awesome! You are brilliant. You slayed!

Write a Letter to Someone Special

So, while I'm happy to be giving you these pep talks, I think it's time you show yourself some compassion. You know, the kind you show everyone else all day every day. Yup, that type of care.

So, I'd like you to write this letter to yourself and read it whenever you may need it.

Dear _____

I am writing this to you to remind you that you were AMAZING, today. I know that it was extremely hard on you when _____

_____

_____

and you felt like _____

_____

But, you got yourself here. Do you know how much fortitude that takes? Do you know how many of these situations you've already persevered through? I am so very proud of you.

With love,
Future Me

Songwriting Activity

    Okay, now you might feel as though I am stretching it, but I know you've got this in you. And, at the very least, we can laugh at ourselves! So, naturally, it's time for songwriting!
    Yes, it's now your turn to write a song!
    (I promise you, I'll sing along!)
    You can do this,
    be an orchestral rebel,
    And I bass this on a guarantee that you won't get in trebel.
    (. . . and this is why we are leaving the songwriting to you.
    Yes, do as I say and not what I crescend-do.)
    Let's start with a warmup, as songwriters do,
    Do, Re, Mi (yes, now it's all about you!)
    Fa, So (have I kept your attention?)
    La Ti Do (you feel a decrease in your tension?)

    Here's where you take over,
    Time for you to write your song.
    Entitled:
    "Twinkle Twinkle Little Mom"
    By the incredible, celebrated
    Twinkle Twinkle Little Mom,
    Who's being forced to write a song.
    I'm feeling _____ and feeling _____
    But that's okay because we can always _____.

    Is your mind still wandering? I could tell. Ok, how's this?

Alphabetize These Words:

Enough
Care
Nurturing
Acceptance
Meditation
Breathing
Dialectical
Inhale
Exhale
Patient
Loving
Extraordinary
LEGO
Charming
Birth
Healthcare
Decisions
Resilience

YOU ROCKED IT! See you again tomorrow night! It's a date!

Chapter 2: They Call Me the Baby Whisperer!

A Boundaries Story

In one arm you hold your swaddled, drowsy baby; in the other, you absentmindedly try to brush your teeth. You're so drained that it feels hard to move the brush up and down, so you rely on the motion from your bouncing and rocking, something you now catch yourself doing while holding the baby and, sometimes, when not holding the baby.

Up and down, back and forth, it works for soothing and for oral hygiene, at least in a pinch.

You're still in your sweatpants (yes—that old pair) and feel really accomplished that you're brushing your teeth before noon. When you used to hear stories of parents who stayed in their pajamas, unshowered and unbrushed, after having a baby, you were skeptical.

"How could someone be so busy that they literally cannot find five minutes to get clean and throw on some athletic wear?" you'd asked yourself. Now, you get it. Sometimes, leaving the baby so you can shower feels daunting. Sometimes, when no one else is home, it feels downright scary.

So, you're skipping showers and celebrating your impeccable oral hygiene.

"I am such a badass!" You say, toothbrush hanging out the side of your mouth, drooling toothpaste so that you have to slurp it back up before it hits your baby in the face.

"And so hot too." At least you still have your sense of humor.

You feel lucky, every day, that you're doing as well as you are. Despite a few days of crying early on, you're coping. You don't feel sad, you're not extraordinarily weepy, and you are able to care for yourself and your baby. If anything, you have been feeling a bit numb. Not in a bad way, just in a "survival" way, perhaps.

Your thoughts are interrupted when you hear the twinkly sound of your phone's ringer and look down on the counter of your bathroom sink. You see the name and stifle a shudder. It's your mom's best friend, the one who has been dying to visit you and the baby. She just loves babies. Babies love her.

"You know, they call me the baby whisperer," she'd told you countless times.

You are tempted to send it to voicemail but know that the pressure to call back will weigh more heavily than getting it over with and picking up the phone. You put down your toothbrush, spit out the extra toothpaste, and press "Accept" on your screen.

"Hiiiii, honey!" The voice trills in a friendly, yet too-loud-for-this-time-of-day way. "I am just in the neighborhood! I'd love to stop by to visit you and the baby! I'm happy to give some snuggles and just help out! You can even use the time to do an errand or have a shower! Either way, I'll just be a half hour, tops!"

You recognize that this is a generous, lovely offer, made with the best of intentions, and, at the same time, it causes your stomach to drop. You freeze up, something that you've been doing more of lately. Someone explained that it's a coping mechanism (fight/flight/freeze) but this offer shouldn't be so scary for you.

"Hi!"

You need a minute. You need a brief window of time to think about what is best for you and your baby.

"Thank you so much for calling," you go on.

"I really appreciate your offer. I just have to figure out a few things, so I will call you back in a couple of minutes."

Already, you've accomplished something. Instead of your go-to, an apology-laced-long-drawn-out explanation, in which you'd ask her permission, you are clear and emphatic.

The old you would have said how sorry you are for the inconvenience, and asked her if waiting two minutes would be okay, please, please, please? You are trying to be more assertive. If not for your sake, then at least for the baby.

It felt unnatural, but you did it, like running a mile in shoes of the wrong size. You are accomplished, albeit uncomfortable. You've started to build the boundaries around yourself and your family. Boundaries don't have to be ominous and impenetrable; rather, they can be clear, mobile, flexible.

No matter what you decide, things will be okay, but you need to get yourself situated. In this moment, your mind is racing as you rock and bounce.

Rock and bounce.

Ruminate and Clear and flexible.

Repeat.

You remind yourself that if someone cannot give you a few minutes then that is their problem, not your problem, and you've made a reasonable request and explained the request clearly. This is not a situation in which a family friend needs help; they are not in peril.

As you rock, you decide you need a little distance from your big feelings, and so you choose to go on the balcony in order to make this decision. By this, you are allowing yourself to take a step back, look at the choice from above, as opposed to being stuck in the mire of it. A little distance, with time and perspective, can bring down the emotions while simultaneously affording clarity. You stand on your metaphorical balcony evaluating the situation below you.

Your clear, mobile, flexible walls are fortifying.

As you challenge yourself and the different factors that will go into making this decision, you try to ask yourself some key questions:

- Who is this visit for?
- Does a visit sound like it will feel intrusive as opposed to a positive distraction?
- Is a spontaneous visit a good way to flex your social muscles?
- Do you want to flex them?

If you know where you want to be, then you can work on how to get there. Whatever you choose, as long as it is in line with your values, which is the well-being of you and your own family, it is the right choice. And regardless of the specifics, you need to set and express clear boundaries.

You attempt to answer your own questions, being as honest as you can be with yourself. You owe yourself that. You deserve it. Regardless of the choice, however, you'll need to continue to set, express, and enforce clear boundaries. You remind yourself that if someone does not accept your boundaries, that is the perfect example of why you needed to create that boundary in the first place.

You think about the acronym you once saw on a poster in your high school guidance counselor's office, and subsequently personalized:

> B—Be honest with yourself
> O—Only you know what is right
> U—Understand where your feelings are coming from
> N—Normalize changing your mind with new facts
> D—Doing what is best for YOU is not selfish
> A—Ask for time, space, and control when needed
> R—Respect others and only accept respect in return
> Y—You've got this!

And so, you are ready to make your decision.

CHOICE POINT: WOULD YOU LIKE TO INVITE YOUR FAMILY FRIEND TO VISIT?

CHOICE 1: If you'd like to allow them to visit, turn to page 41.
CHOICE 2: If choose to decline the offer for a visit, turn to page 43.

CHOICE 1: You allow them to visit.

You take a deep breath, splash some cold water on your face, and sigh audibly.

These days, every decision seems momentous, which only serves to make you more indecisive. You decide to let her visit, but on your terms. In order to stand your ground in a situation that could instinctually cause you to freeze, you mentally construct a boundary around yourself and the baby. You build something clear, so that you can hear and see through it, but solid enough to shield you from that with which you are not comfortable.

You open your call log to "recents" and dial your family friend.

"Soooo???" The voice trills, skipping the traditional greeting.

You steady yourself, armed with a clear answer, solid boundaries, and all of the self-respect this time has afforded to you.

"Thank you so much for calling," you begin.

"We'd love to have you over! But I just want to set up expectations from the beginning: the baby eats in a half hour, and during that time I need the house to be totally quiet and free from distractions, so it will have to be a quick visit. If you'd prefer a longer visit and more quality time, we can schedule another time in advance! Would you like to come now for about twenty minutes?"

You've been clear, established a manageable time-limit, and know you can handle twenty minutes of annoyance, though you suspect you might be pleasantly surprised.

You don't know how she will respond, but you hope that, as the baby whisperer, she will understand the importance of these guidelines. And, if not, you do. That's all that really matters.

You've tackled a hard decision, stretched a bit out of your comfort zone, while managing to act consistently with your most important values. This is a win. And, no matter what else happens today, no matter how many times you are peed on, or chewed on, or not able to shower, you've done this.

And sometimes, one small victory is enough.

Congratulations! You've Collected Coping Mechanism Badge of Boundaries Boss.

Turn to page 46 to return to the story.

CHOICE 2: You decline her offer to visit.

You take a deep breath, splash some cold water on your face, and sigh audibly.

These days, every decision seems momentous, which only serves to make you more indecisive.

You open your call log to "recents" and dial your family friend.

"Soooo???" The voice trills, skipping the traditional greeting.

You steady yourself, armed with a clear answer, solid boundaries, and all of the self-respect this time has afforded to you.

"Thank you so much for calling," you begin.

"I'm sorry, but now is not a good time for a visit. We would love to have you over, but the baby eats in a half hour, and during that time I need the house to be totally quiet and free from distractions, so I'd prefer to be able to have some quality time with you. Can we schedule a time now for a longer visit? How about next Sunday?"

You've been clear, established a manageable expectation, while also making her feel prioritized. You don't know how she will respond, but you hope that, as the baby whisperer, she will understand the importance of your boundaries. And, if not, you do. That's all that matters.

It wasn't an easy decision. But the house is a mess, you are a mess, everything feels out of control, and the idea of someone holding the baby right now is not only not helpful, it feels yucky.

You remember your doula's wise words about this crucial postpartum period, and how you need proper time to recover and heal. This is your time to rest, bond with the baby, nourish yourself, and essentially stay in a little cocoon. Sometimes the hard choice is also the right choice.

As soon as she speaks, you know that she isn't going to take this perceived slight lightly.

"Are you sure I can't just stop by for a few minutes? I can even feed the baby for you, because I know your aunt came last week, and she keeps talking about it."

Ugh, you groan to yourself, silently in your head, as though you can hear your own voice. *Since when is it not okay to change our minds? Can we normalize the fact that we are all just humans and our thoughts cannot—really, should not—be etched in stone?"*

It always astonished you that people weren't expected to immediately fit back into their pre-pregnancy jeans, yet parents were expected to fit back into their pre-parenthood minds.

Yes, you had your aunt visit last week and yes, it was fine, and yes, today is different. You stick to your script, repeating yourself in a way that is gentle and not patronizing.

"I am so sorry that today doesn't work for a visit. We really appreciate your call and would love to schedule something for next week."

It takes a few more times but, finally, and not without more protest, you get off the phone.

Along with the relief you feel, you also feel an unexpected heaviness in your stomach, which you realize is the physical manifestation of vulnerability. When you first set new boundaries, it can feel hard, and as though you've done something wrong. But, though you feel like you've unzipped yourself and are walking around without your outer layer of skin, this is all part of the process.

Saying "no" or potentially disappointing someone has always been really hard for you. "It's always hard to do hard things," you say to your baby, but, you suspect, really to yourself. "But that's how they get easier." This is a win.

You've tackled a hard decision, stretched a bit out of your comfort zone, while managing to act consistently with your most important values. And, no matter what else happens today, no matter how many times you are peed on, or chewed on, or not able to shower, you've done this. And sometimes, one small victory is enough.

Congratulations! You've Collected Coping Mechanism Badge of *Persistent Protector*.

Turn to page 46 to return to the story.

BONUS: Set Your Boundaries

When we speak of boundaries, we are referring to the limits and guidelines and space between ourselves and the people, places, and things in our lives. Boundaries are as varied as they are vital. They can be internal or external, solid or permeable, physical or emotional, just to name a few. Because they are so salient, we are going to use this space to practice identifying, naming, and fortifying our boundaries. Here we go!

Boundary Circles

Boundary circles are a great way to identify our proximity to the people and things in our lives. If we picture ourselves at the center of our concentric circles, then the smaller circle next to us is where we keep those allowed to impact us most. The closer someone is to your core, the more access they can have on your life. Who and what is allowed to get close to you is entirely up to you. You control your own boundaries.

Fill in your own boundary circles and keep this activity close, to use when you need a little reminder of who and what is allowed to affect you.

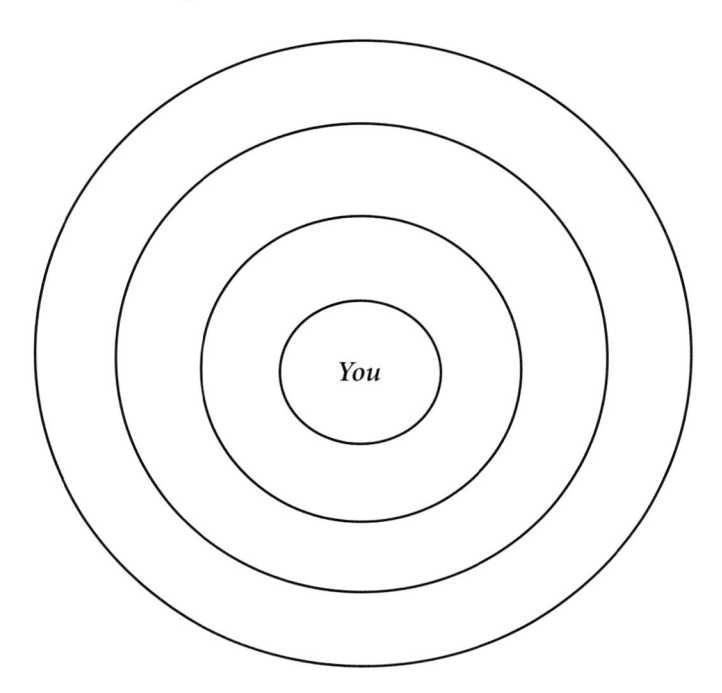

Create Your Own Boundary Acronym

Here is another example, and then it will be time for yours!

B—Believe in your inherent self-worth
O—Offer simple explanations
U—Understanding your own motivations is enough
N—No one can tell you how you should feel
D—Doing something more often makes it easier
A—Anyone who is really "your person" will . . .
R—Respect your boundary, even if it is hard or inconvenient
Y—You've got this!

Let's see what you've got!

B—
O—
U—
N—
D—
A—
R—
Y—

Visualize or Sketch Yourself

First, think of a boundary you'd like to create. This can be an internal boundary (think of your feelings, thoughts, and emotions) or an external boundary (think of your physical being, personal space, or amount of time). Name this boundary.

Next, draw a picture of yourself with the boundary in place and without the boundary in place. This may help you to discover how you truly feel about the situation. Visualizing yourself will make decisions and actions easier.

With the boundary | **Without the boundary**

Chapter 3: Smiling While You Are Simply Surviving

A Communication Story

"Hiiiiiiiiii!"

Never before has the word sounded so jarring.

You turn your head, adjusting your sunglasses to get a better look, and feel walloped by the site of her:

Your neighbor: a fellow new parent, standing less than a foot away from you, smartly dressed, smiling brightly, in the same supermarket aisle.

This is exactly what you were dreading and the very reason why, when you realized in horror that you had to make this quick trip to the grocery, you stuffed your dirty hair into a baseball cap, grabbed your oversized sunglasses, and made a beeline for the baby aisle.

A good parent wouldn't have run out of formula in the first place, you'd mentally admonished yourself. *A good parent would have realized it sooner.*

In truth, it was a miscommunication, but you were still feeling awful about the mix-up. And, despite feeling awful, you had to remedy the problem, which meant said trip to the grocery, when, of course, (because why wouldn't this happen to you?) you'd been spotted by a neighbor. Not just any neighbor. This neighbor.

"OMG! Hiiiiiiii!" She repeats, as you struggle to get your bearings.

You never feel your best these days, but with this person as your foil, you feel downright sheepish: she is light where you are dark; kempt where you are straggly; smiling where you are simply surviving.

You don't know each other well, but, incredibly, you both had your babies in the same hospital, on the same floor, on the very same day. You can conjure the memory like it was yesterday.

"Can you believe it?!" she had chirped, as you stood, side-by-side, outside the hospital's nursery. "We are TWINNING!"

At the time, the notion had seemed comical; things seemed funnier then, in general. She had been in a flowy, flowery caftan, her hair looking freshly blown-out, her skin glowing, her baby sleeping soundly. At that particular moment, your breasts were leaking through your faded, cotton hospital gown at the sound of your wailing newborn.

"Hi. Yes. Well, I don't usually leave the baby in the nursery, it's just that they told me to take a nap, and that they had to do some tests, so . . . " you stammer, excuses, though rationally, you knew that this woman was there for the exact same reason you were. Somehow, you felt as though you were doing something wrong.

Somehow, you feel the same way now.

"Hi, how are you?" you try to make conversation, but the words feel sandy and acrid coming out of your mouth. You wonder when simple communication had become so hard. *Why can't I be normal? What is wrong with me?* you ask yourself, silently.

"Goooood. You know!" she smiles as she replies. She is warm and friendly, but it feels intrusive. Aggressively kind.

You wonder what she thinks you know.

You stand there for an extra beat, suddenly forgetting the sole reason you found yourself in this awful place at this awful time.

"I have been meaning to text you!" she says as she gets closer to you. She smells clean and flowery. You don't even want to think about how you must smell, as you'd grabbed the nearest shirt, thrown it on, and had neglected to check it for spit-up residue or pit stains. She stands on her tiptoes to peek over your shoulder at the containers of formula, neatly arranged on the shelves behind you. You begin to silently panic, as you're about to be found out.

She's going to know that your baby is formula-fed and that you couldn't even remember to do the simple task of keeping said formula in the house, because you do everything wrong, your inner voice says.

She's going to know that you had planned to exclusively nurse for six months, and couldn't even make it a month, even though you tried your hardest, because the baby had trouble latching and your nipples were being torn up. She's going to know that you're a failure. Your mind races, a carousel of fears spinning as you hop from scary-thought-horse to scary-thought-horse.

But, to your surprise, she picks up a container of formula—the same one that you've filled your cart with—and makes a "hmmm" sound.

"Do you like this kind? I just buy whatever is on sale," she laughs at herself. Is it possible that she's not judging but, rather, endearing?

She uses formula? Your inner voice questions, scarcely believing the thought.

"Yes," you stammer. "I do. I did a lot of research and this one has been gentle on the baby's tummy."

She plucks a container from the shelf and flashes another warm smile.

"You're sooo good," she offers praise easily. "The only research I do these days is about my stretch marks. I love my child, but she really did mangle my body." She holds up her T-shirt to show her bare stomach, which, of course, looks exactly how a postpartum stomach should look.

She should see my stomach, you think.

"You look great," you say, trying to mirror her warmth as you feel yourself starting to sweat.

"You're the sweetest. Did you ever think you'd be so comfortable talking about the color and textures of baby poop while in public, as though it's perfectly normal conversation?"

You note that she seems to have gotten the subtext of the "gentle on the baby's tummy" and ponder the notion that you're not the only one experiencing potential dairy allergies and definite poop-splosions.

Your mental carousel ride is interrupted as she smiles and says, "So, I've totally been meaning to text you. I am starting a baby play group at my house. It will be every Wednesday from, like, 12–2, but come for as long or as short as you want!

Heck, come in your pajamas! I don't usually get out of mine until dinner time anyway. Parenthood, amiright? So, can you join?"

You're surprised; not by the invitation, but by your realization: this person is not only nice, but she's normal. She's someone you might even choose to be friends with. She's honest and self-deprecating and seems authentic. You remind yourself to stop being so judgmental.

You love being a parent. You love baby things. You're tempted by her offer. You just have no desire to interact with other people, unless they're your family members (and even that can be iffy) or on your television screen (they, of course, can be powered off).

So, despite the fact that you like this person, you freeze at the thought of a real, regular, time-contingent, clothing-contingent plan. You haven't done those. Not since giving birth, at least. You used to be a total planner, with your days mapped out on a color-coded schedule. Having a baby changes everything. Suddenly, a schedule doesn't just seem impossible, it feels downright scary.

You collect yourself.

"That's so nice. Thank you so much for thinking of us!" You begin. You want her to know how deeply you appreciate her offer.

You struggle with your reply. You feel torn. On one hand, you know that getting to know her and other parents would be good for you and the baby. But it feels so overwhelming. You don't want to miss this opportunity, and you don't want to commit to something that will only weigh on you.

You're granted a reprieve when her cell phone rings.

"So sorry, I have to just take this, I'll be right back!"

You breathe a momentary sigh of relief, but your mind starts to fill with negative self-talk once more.

You can almost see the thought bubbles above your head, hanging over you like a character in a graphic novel. You don't want to let your fear make the decision for you, so you attempt to pop the thought bubbles one by one.

> *I have a harder time than other parents making plans.*
> Pop!
> *My baby would be better off if I were a different type of parent.*
> Pop!
> *I still look pregnant, and I don't want other people to see me.*
> Pop!
> *This should be easier.*
> Pop! Pop! Pop!

This exercise has helped. It's not a cure-all, but it has allowed you to lower the temperature of things.

You try your best to be mindful in this moment, free from distraction, which, in the current circumstance, is not an easy feat. No matter what you decide to do, you are at least going to try to make the decision with a clear(ish) head and with abundant grace for your postpartum self.

So, with the bubbles temporarily popped, and before they can reanimate, you decide to try something. Instead of acting based on pure emotion, you use the technique of observe and describe.

First, you take a moment to observe how you're feeling. You remind yourself not to editorialize or make judgements: you're simply observing, so when the word "overwhelmed" dances across your thoughts, you shake it from your head; you're just observing, not judging.

> *My hands are shaking a tiny bit, like I just had an energy drink, but I'm simultaneously exhausted. My chest feels a little tight and a little heavy.*

You take a few deep breaths, something that always helps to calm your body when you are feeling revved up, just in time for your friend to return.

"So sorry, again! It was the pediatrician's office. Would you believe I forgot to schedule her next appointment? I swear, this parent-brain thing is real! So, can you join us on Wednesday?"

CHOICE POINT: DO YOU ACCEPT HER OFFER?

CHOICE 1: If you choose to accept her offer, turn to page 57.
CHOICE 2: If you choose to decline her offer, turn to page 58.

CHOICE 1: You choose to accept the offer.

Mustering up your strength, heart beating quickly, you decide to open yourself up a bit. You're not used to being so vulnerable, especially in public, and especially with someone new, but parenthood has transformed you in all ways, and so you're trying this on for size.

"I really appreciate your offer. Seriously, thanks for including me. This new-parent thing is harder than I thought, so it would be great to meet some other parents with babies the same age. The thing is, we haven't gotten out much lately. I feel like every time we make a plan, the baby changes the whole schedule, and every time we are headed out the door, the baby spits up all over his cute outfit."

"That's okay!" She interjects. "We are all in it together."

From her, it doesn't sound trite; it sounds true.

"I might be late or have to cancel at the last minute, and we might be covered in bodily fluids, but we will be there. What can we bring?"

Without another word she embraces you, in a tight, warm hug.

"Thank you," she says, her voice brimming with emotion.

"I'm so glad I'm not the only one. I think you and I are going to be really good friends."

With that, you finalize plans, say your goodbyes, and head to the register.

Your heart—and cart—are full.

Congratulations! You've Collected Coping Mechanism Badge of *Outstanding Observer*.

Turn to page 60 to return to the story.

CHOICE 2: You choose to decline the offer.

Mustering up your strength, heart beating quickly, you decide to open up a bit. You're not used to being so vulnerable, especially in public, and especially with someone new, but parenthood has transformed you in all ways, and so you're trying this on for size.

"I really appreciate your offer. Seriously, thanks for including me. This new-parent thing is harder than I thought, so it would be great to meet some other parents with babies the same age. The thing is, we haven't gotten out much lately. I feel like every time we make a plan, the baby changes the schedule, and every time we are headed out the door, the baby spits up all over his cute outfit."

"That's okay!" She interjects. "We are all in it together." From her, it doesn't sound trite; it sounds true.

"Right now, I feel like having something on the calendar will make me feel pressured—totally self-imposed, you haven't made me feel that way at all—so I think we will wait until he's a little older and we are a bit more settled. But I really mean it, we will get there. It may just take us a bit more time."

Without another word she embraces you, in a tight, warm hug.

"Thank you," she says, her voice brimming with emotion.

"Thank you for being so honest. When did saying 'no' become so hard!? Everything feels hard, and I'm so glad I'm not the only one who feels this way. This is all so much harder than they say. I don't know how I'm going to pull this off, but fake it till you make it, right? The door is always open for you. And, if the group feels too overwhelming, can we make an always-tentative-fully-cancel-able-spontaneous coffee date?"

"That would be great." You really mean it. "I think you and I are going to be really good friends."

With that, you say your goodbyes and head to the register. Your heart—and cart—are full.

Congratulations! You've Collected Coping Mechanism Badge of *Outstanding Observer*.

Turn to page 60 to return to the story.

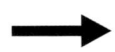

BONUS: Pop Your Negative Thought Bubbles

First, fill these spaces with as many negative thoughts as you are experiencing. It's okay to leave room for later woes or to add more of your own! Anything goes.

Once you've filled the bubbles, you can, one by one, pop them. Just like that! Cross them off, scribble all over them, do whatever feels soothing in that moment. More will come, as they always do, but you know how to handle them.

You're taking control and getting rid of that which does not serve you. Have at it!

THE KID STORIES

In which we discuss:
Planning Ahead
Judgment
Support

Chapter 4: Tired in Your Bones

A Planning-Ahead Story

The light is streaming in through a small crack in the blinds. Shadows shaped like diamonds dance across your bedroom wall welcoming the new day.

The sky is like sherbet. You're still wrapped up in a not-quite-dreamy-yet-not-quite-awake state of consciousness. As your thoughts begin to clear, you hear your old favorite song playing from the small speaker of your iPhone.

You've been meaning to change that. It's amazing how something so wonderful can morph into something so dreaded, simply by dressing up as an alarm. Morning has come, and you are still exhausted. Wiped. Tired in your bones.

You're in a new phase of parenthood. You no longer have diapers or bottles or nap schedules to wrestle with. Now, you are the parent of kids. Kids with sticky hands, boundless energy, and strong wills.

You love every inch of their sticky hands, boundless energy, and strong wills, even when it's not so easy to enjoy those things. They make life so much more vibrant, and it feels like a privilege to see things through their eyes. You didn't realize how long it had been since you had stopped to look at the little, normal, commonplace things with such wonder.

And, you have to admit that life with kids is both so much better and so much more challenging than you could have ever imagined. There are inane arguments, explosive tantrums, and epic messes. There are toys that no one will touch for years but which, as soon as one child decides to use it, suddenly becomes the most important object on earth, causing meltdowns of enormous proportions. There are meals ruined over the color of a cup and nights ruined over the wrong bedtime story.

Then, there are the sweet times, when your children astonish you with their empathy, compassion, and wisdom; when they use new words, learn new skills, and grow new inches; when they help one another and, more importantly, themselves; and when they're independent, innovative, and inspiring.

You mediate when your kids are fighting and melt when they're showing each other love. Being a parent is all the things. And, managing all the things, and feeling all the things, leaves you tired. So, so tired.

As your alarm continues to sound and the sky continues to lighten, you realize you have a choice to make: to wake or to snooze.

It seems like an easy decision, but it's not. It never is. Do you prioritize sleep or free time? Which makes you a better parent? A better human? Can you be both?

CHOICE POINT: DO YOU WANT TO WAKE UP NOW?

CHOICE 1: If you decide to snooze the alarm, turn to page 64.
CHOICE 2: If you decide to wake up in that moment, turn to page 67.

CHOICE 1: You decide to hit snooze.

You peek at your phone, avoiding as much of the blue-light as you can, and notice the title of your alarm: SLEEP=WELLNESS. You'd planned ahead.

You press the button for the SLEEP=WELLNESS alarm, giving yourself an extra thirty minutes.

As hard as it can be to accept sleep is so important. Especially in this phase of things where your kids are old enough to run—but not old enough to run by themselves all day. With enough rest (though, is there ever enough rest?), you'll be better equipped to tackle the challenges ahead, even if it means you miss out on any peaceful alone time before you have to pivot into parent-mode.

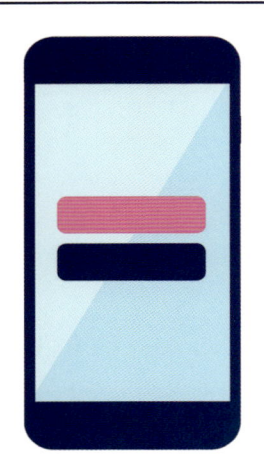

You know that for some, sleep is the most important thing, and, while for others, solace is most important. While you wish you could have both, in this moment, getting some rest will be the healthiest choice for both your body and your brain. This is why you've planned ahead.

You've created a routine for yourself, but, like most things, there has been a steep learning curve. By prioritizing sleep and arranging your mornings to do so, you miss out on other things. You've learned parenthood has changed all things physically, emotionally, and logistically. In your daily life, you no longer have alone time, with the house quiet and light low. You no longer have the freedom to eat breakfast without little fingers grabbing for your cream of wheat or chocolate croissant or, in the darkest of times, coffee.

You no longer have time to check every box of the to-do list before heading out for the day. Things remain unnoticed, unfinished, undone. It feels selfish to prioritize your own rest over all of these other things, but you're trying to make more of an effort to do so.

It's something you've been working on. In the past, you used to try to get up and shout half-hearted offers from under the duvet. "I'll get up . . ." you'd say, trying to convince yourself as much as others.

Then, there was the, regrettably, passive-aggressive phase, when you'd exclaim, "No, you don't have to get up. I can do it. Just give me a few minutes. I'm still sooooo tired."

The problem is that people, sometimes, associate sleep with laziness and you suffer from no one's judgment more than your own.

You are so hard on yourself.

You're trying to be better about it, but you're also trying not to be too hard on yourself for being so hard on yourself. You were once called out for apologizing for apologizing. You've been trying to be a better self-advocate.

So, you set an alarm that serves as a reminder, in shorthand, that you need sleep. Even when you don't feel like you (though you arguably do) deserve it.

This morning, this extra time to rest is a blessing, as always. Your heavy eyes close once more, sinking deeper into your cozy covers. It can be hard to go back to sleep in these moments, and you need every moment of rest, so you rely on a body scan to help. It's been part of your new effort. Sometimes, you fall back to sleep right away, but on days like today, you need this helpful tool.

Starting with the tip of your toes, you slowly, deliberately, relax each part of your body, letting go of every drop of tension. You guide yourself through this exercise, as you've practiced it, and are a pro.

You relax your toes.

Then, you relax your feet.

Then, you relax your heels.

Then, you relax your ankles. Let them just sink into the bed.

Your entire body from the ankles-down is completely, totally relaxed, like you're melting into the sheets.

Next, you relax your calves.

Relax your knees . . .

And, before you can go any further up your body, before any more boxes are checked or pastries are swiped or negotiations are made or apologies are uttered . . . you've drifted back off to sleep.

Congratulations! You've Collected Coping Mechanism Badge of *Mindful Mapper.*

Turn to page 74 to return to the story.

CHOICE 2: You decide to wake up in that moment.

As you start to wake up, both mentally and physically, you peek at your phone and notice the title of your alarm.

SOLACE=WELLNESS. You'd planned ahead.

You turn off your alarm and shake the last remnants of sleep from your head.

As hard as it can be to accept, for you, this alone time is so important. With enough time (though, is there ever enough time?), you'll be better equipped to tackle the day ahead, even if it means you miss out on a little more sleep. You prefer your alone-time to be spent while you are conscious, as opposed to unconscious, though you can appreciate the need for both sleep and alone time.

You know that for some, sleep is the most important thing, and, while for others, solace is most important. While you wish you had time to accomplish both things, getting some time to yourself will be the healthiest choice for both your body and your brain. This is why you've planned ahead.

SUB-CHOICE POINT: Do you want to get out of bed?

SUB-CHOICE 1: If you choose to get up and out of bed, turn to page 68.
SUB-CHOICE 2: If you choose to wake up but stay in bed, turn to page 71.

SUB-CHOICE 1: Getting out of bed

You wish you could stay under the covers, but you can't, so you accept it. You've planned ahead and snuggle into the comfort of your daily ritual instead of struggling through a sea of guilt and worry.

You rub your eyes and rub your fingers through your tangled hair as you notice the lightening sky. It looks like it will be a beautiful day.

You've created a routine for yourself, but, like most things, there has been a steep learning curve. By prioritizing this time, and arranging your mornings to do so, you miss out on other things—mainly, sleep.

So, you savor the things that are most important to you in this phase of your life: a little bit of sweet, sweet alone time, with the house quiet and light low; the freedom to eat breakfast without little fingers grabbing for your cream of wheat or chocolate croissant or coffee.

You have a bit of time to decide whether you want to try to check every box of the to-do list before heading out for the day. Or not. But it's your choice.

You follow the components of your morning ritual, feeling grateful for this time of quiet, solace, and, truthfully, freedom. No one else needs to be fed, brushed, washed, or dressed . . . this is your moment to take care of yourself. You start to feel guilty about needing this alone time, wondering to yourself if other parents are better parents, if they don't crave time to themselves.

You pour yourself a cup of coffee, smiling at the misshapen mug (reading "World's Best Parent") which you know makes everything taste a little more delicious. You've prepared for this moment, so, on the page with your long to-do list, you read the little, hand-written printed piece of paper you've stuck in there. Your personal pep talk:

You crave routine. You yearn for control. You know this about yourself. But forgiveness and flexibility are essential. Life is mercurial and things happen. When you get stuck on a routine, you're not setting yourself up for a win. And you deserve a win! You're you, after all. Also, for those with any anxiety (ahem), you may attribute these moments of change as signs or, worse, warnings. These feelings are you grasping for control, but they aren't real. There is no relationship between how much you believe something is true and how true it is.

Did you get that?

There is no relationship between how strongly, deeply, fiercely you believe something is true and how true it is. So, if you always plan ahead by setting your coffee machine to brew your dark roast for you at promptly 6:11 a.m. and you wake up to find the machine—and your spirits—unplugged and lightless, that sucks! How annoying! But is it a sign that your day is going to be terrible or that scary things are to come? Nope. Someone knocked the plug out of the wall. It happens. You can handle it.

You think back to the morning when you wrote yourself this pep talk. You'd been feeling peaceful and wanted to give yourself a boost during the times when things were a little more chaotic. This pep talk note, while seemingly silly, is an important message and a strong way to start your day.

By the time the kids start to plod down the stairs asking for food and clothing and for all of their needs to be met, because apparently, they are incapable of meeting their own needs before eight o'clock in the morning, you're already in a calm, intentional, purposeful place. It doesn't mean that things won't get hard, but you know that you can handle hard; you can handle anything.

Congratulations! You've Collected Coping Mechanism Badge of *Pep-Talk Prodigy*.

Turn to page 74 to return to the story.

SUB-CHOICE 2: Staying in bed

You peek at your phone, avoiding as much of the blue light as you can, and notice the title of your alarm: SOLACE=WELLNESS. You'd planned ahead.

And yet, you're up. You know that sleep is healing, wish that you had more time to engage in the practice, but accept that it is not always realistic.

And, as if on cue, you hear the familiar melody of little feet running, your bedroom door creaking, and your name—or, rather, title—being called. Even in this moment, you recognize that it's the best title you could ever have.

Your kids have a habit of addressing you as though you are not only wide awake, but mid-conversation, no matter how deeply you are sleeping. There is a difference between being up and being *up for this*. You're awake, even if it is begrudgingly, and yet not ready to engage in deep conversations about TV characters or transcendentalism.

You make a choice, in this moment, and one that is hard to admit to endorsing, even to yourself. Those are the most difficult of choices. Before announcing your plan, you remind yourself of a dialectical truth, which means that two things can be equally true at the same time:

Your mental health is best when you are acting in a way that honors your values.

And there is always room for grace.

You think of a piece of advice you'd heard recently, on a particularly inspiring podcast. It was all about the delicate balance of structure and flexibility, and all the things that can disrupt the balance and all of the ways to regain control. The line you've been holding on to still rings clear and strong in your head:

There is no relationship between how much you believe something is true and how true it is.

Armed with that knowledge and an iPad, you float an offer to your child. You begin with your standard, not-even-the-sun-has-made-up-its-mind-yet greeting.

"Good morning, my love! How did you sleep?" You and your little one exchange warm, morning pleasantries and express your adoration, which, sometimes, is done without any words at all.

"Hey, can I tell you the truth? I am feeling really tired this morning. I think I need a little time for myself before I get up with you."

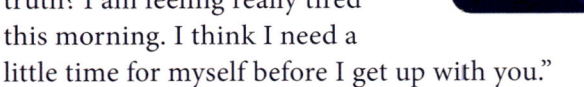

At first, you see a little face fall a bit. You swoop back in with, "So, I'd like you to take this iPad from me and you can watch or play on the PBS Kids app until I get up in about ten minutes. It may be a bit longer, but I will be right here. If you get hungry, there are granola bars and fruit pouches in the pantry."

Your child's face, now brighter than the early sky, indicates your success.

As you watch the cute, pajama-clad kid scamper away, carrying an iPad and sense of autonomy, you remind yourself that you're doing the right thing by meeting your needs for this brief moment. Your child is safe, fed, and learning something from Daniel Tiger, no doubt.

Though you're not 100 percent confident, you've committed to this plan, and so you flip over onto your belly, open your phone, and check your favorite website. Do you feel guilty? The tiniest bit. You ask yourself why. Is your child disappointed? Or are you carrying the yuckiness for no reason but your own.

You exhale, remind yourself that you're doing a great job, and find a pleasant way to waste your time as you savor your ten minutes of cozy, covered bliss.

Congratulations! You've Collected Coping Mechanism Badge of *Dialectical Dynamo*.

Turn to page 74 to return to the story.

BONUS: Prep Your Own Pep Talk

Write your own pep talk note to get you off to a good start each day. Post it on your mirror or as the wallpaper on your phone.

Chapter 5: Blackbeard is Mushy Food Intolerant

A Judgment Story

For one moment, the world around you feels quiet. From your post at the kitchen sink, you notice all of the little morning sounds. The drip, drip, drip of the coffee; the birds conversing from perches in the trees; the garbage truck rumbling by. And, as quickly as you'd noticed it, the peacefulness is disrupted by the sound of a stampede.

"How can humans that are so little make a noise so loud?" You ask yourself, not for the first time.

That one, precious morning vignette will have to sustain you, as you know that at any moment you will begin the familiar dance of dining and driving and dishwashing, oh my.

Morning is a time you always anticipate with both delight and dread.

Mealtimes, diet, nutrition, feeding, the whole general topic is a thing. Ironically, it's one of those things that everyone tells you not to make into a thing and yet, it is. You've been intentional about the what and the how of feeding your kids. You have avoided the power struggles and the black-and-white thinking—the food rules and the pressures. You are all about moderation, and it suits you most of the time. Sometimes, however, it can be really stressful.

You constantly feel like other parents have it together in a way that, despite your best efforts, you do not. You see so many posts online and on social media from moms sharing all about their . . .

Five-year-old with a sophisticated palate, who particularly loves experimental umami cuisine.

Or

Organic produce, which they grow on their own sustainable farm and live off of.

Or

Magic ability to turn spinach into Sour Patch Kids.

Not only does your pantry lack 100 percent-pure spinach gummies, but also your kids have questionable table manners, sometimes require electronics at the table when out to dinner, and if you told them about something "experimental and umami" they would laugh and say, "Ew!! Mommy!!"

Your thoughts are interrupted as your kids appear. And, as if on cue, your kids assume their positions in the *morning dance*, emerging with groggy grumbles. They're sleepy and hungry and your aim is to get them fed as soon as possible. Fuel helps.

"Good morning!" you greet each other, which is the family equivalent of *first position*.

CHOICE POINT: HOW WOULD YOU LIKE TO OFFER BREAKFAST FOR YOUR KIDS?

CHOICE 1: If you'd like to ask an open-ended, "What would you like for breakfast?", turn to page 78.

CHOICE 2: If you offer your kids a choice between three different options, turn to page 83.

CHOICE 1: You ask an open-ended question.

"What would you like for breakfast?" You repeat as your kids assume their positions at the breakfast table. Heads still bed-like, eyes still glazed over.

As you process that idea, you chew on the word. Glazed. Which leads you to another word. Donuts. Glazed donuts sound particularly tasty to you this morning. But what would the brigade of sugar-free Instagram influencers think? You shudder at the thought!

You snap back to attention when one of your kids' heads goes CLUNK on the table, with dramatic flair. Quite the choreography!

"I don't know," they say through the crook of their elbow.

Your other child does not even respond, distracted by the map they have started trying to secure to the inside of their newly constructed Blackbeard pirate LEGO office.

"Hey, kiddos? What can I get for you? We have twenty minutes until we have to leave." You say, opening the fridge to stare at its familiar contents.

"What do we have?" the kids ask in an ill-timed chorus of sorts.

"We have some cut-up fruit. How about some berries and Greek yogurt?" You float this, hoping for the best, expecting the likely.

"Ew," your younger child says, waving the tiny hook hand on LEGO Blackbeard.

"Okay, I will take that as a 'no thank you,'" you always try to model kindness and polite manners of speaking, though you're tempted to be snarky.

"Can I have cereal?" tries your older kid, relief washing over you as one, small problem has now been solved.

"Sure! We have Rice Krispies, Corn Chex," you start to rattle off the names of grains and their corresponding shapes.

"Fruity Pebbles with extra milk," they perk up as they mention their favorite rainbow-hued breakfast treat.

"Yes," you think to yourself, feeling as though you've just won a tiny, internal battle. You pivot back to the pantry with the grace of a trained professional and grab the familiar red box. Except, it's awfully light. You realize, with horror, that it's been put back empty.

There are no more Fruity Pebbles.

You're about to break the news to your child, crushing their pre-nine o'clock a.m.-dreams, when you remember a line that had been repeated to you since it was first presented as a mantra in your lactation class, back when your kids were infants:

"Fed is best."

Though the phrase is used to assuage parents of the guilt they feel when they feed their babies with formula as opposed to breastmilk, the message still applies, you reason. When it comes down to it, the *only* thing that matters is that the baby (or, in this case, grumpy humans) are fed.

You conjure up the mental image of those donuts once again.

"Who wants to have a car picnic?" You ask before you can psych yourself out of it. You see their faces flush with color and light.

They know what this means: a drive-through breakfast!

And then the dreaded moment of mental admonishment hits you. "Am I the worst parent for not giving them a home-cooked breakfast? Isn't it the most important meal of the day? I thought good parents make hot meals," you think to yourself as you begin to ruminate.

Without being asked, your kids get up from the table, put on their shoes and coats, and head to the door. They are never this cooperative or proactive. It's amazing what happens when pink icing and rainbow sprinkles are introduced into the equation. You file this anecdote away for later.

You see a mental montage of social media parents with rainbows of fresh produce and elaborate dishes packed so that they resemble characters' faces, constructed within the confines of little lunchboxes.

"You're not making a mistake," you coach yourself. "You're making memories."

You get behind the wheel and drive your kids, who have, miraculously, become friends. There is no fighting or fussing. Another piece of evidence for the file. Not that you're promoting food-related bribery, to the contrary, you're noting what these kids are capable of.

As you drive, you continue to acknowledge, and then let go of, the negative thoughts. Instead of beating yourself up, you opt for a mindful drive.

You try to simply focus on the present.

You keep your eyes on the road ahead, really taking in the view. You note the feel of the leather steering wheel under your hands. The weight of the car. The way it feels when the air rushes from the vent and tickles your face. The sound of your kids interacting in a way that doesn't involve brawling, tattletaling, or tears. You root yourself in the present, which calms both your body and your mind.

"It's amazing how much mindfulness you can cram into one, short car ride," you think.

By the time you pull up to the drive-through window, you have replaced the flipbook of images in your head, trading self-criticism for honest perspective. You order a breakfast sandwich and a donut for each of the kids. Hey, you're covering more food groups than you'd expected. Look at you! You order a coffee and a donut for yourself. You don't typically indulge like this, but, in this moment, it feels appropriate to feel part of things—plus, glazed donuts are delicious!

As you park the car and peek into the back seat, you see smiles and contentment, and sometimes, that is just what you need. Plus, you realize that this is just one meal. In the scheme of things, it doesn't really matter.

"The kids are happy," you remind yourself. "This is fun. We are making their morning more exciting."

And, most importantly,
Fed is best.

Congratulations! You've Collected Coping Mechanism Badge of *Tranquil Traveler*.

Turn to page 88 to return to the story.

CHOICE 2: You offer clear choices.

"What would you like for breakfast?" You begin as your kids assume their positions at the breakfast table. Heads still bed-like, eyes still glazed over.

You snap back to attention when one of your kids' heads goes CLUNK on the table, with dramatic flair. Quite the choreography!

"You have three choices to decide from," you continue. This is what you do every morning. You make sure to keep the routine consistent, but the options fresh. You know, just to keep them guessing.

"You can have Greek yogurt with berries, oatmeal with brown sugar, or a bagel with cream cheese."

"Ugh," the kids groan, in an ill-timed chorus of sorts.

"I'm so sick of bagels and berries and oats," your older child continues.

"Blackbeard is mushy food intolerant," your younger child says, waving the tiny hook hand on the LEGO pirate they've been fiddling with.

"Please remind Blackbeard that our oats are steel-cut and therefore free of any mushiness. These are the choices, and I appreciate all of you, pirates included, choosing from one of these three things." You always try to model kindness and polite manners of speaking, though you're tempted to be snarky.

"Can I have eggs?" your older child asks. "I have *such* a craving!"

"Not this morning." The wave of guilt washes over you before you've even finished the sentence. You'd been trying to be so on top of things. You did exactly what your pediatrician had advised by offering three, clear, balanced choices. And, yet, it still isn't enough. You feel terrible that your kid wants a hot breakfast, and, for many reasons, you can't make it for them. Even if you had the time, you reconcile, it wouldn't be the right message. This isn't the time or place to bend. Even though they have *such* a craving.

You chastise yourself silently for being so boring and rigid. For never quite having it right. You peer into the stocked pantry, filled with items that your kids were obsessed with one day only to reject the very next day (after, of course, you'd already bought cases of the fruit leather and seaweed and granola bars).

You step away from the seaweed, muster up your composure, and repeat the choices.

"Greek yogurt, oatmeal, or bagel?" you ask. You can feel your patience-tank emptying.

"Fine," your older child sulks. "I'll have the yogurt. No blueberries, just strawberries, and no squishy ones."

"I don't like any of these things," your younger child complains. "I'm not eating them."

This kind of proclamation is your kryptonite. You know how important fuel is for your kid, both for their energy and also for their mood. You don't want either of them to feel hungry *or* hangry.

You try not to give your younger kid too much attention for this defiance, as you know that is exactly what they're looking for, and you don't want to send the wrong message. A teacher once advised you that when you give a child attention when they act out, it is like handing them 100-dollar bills for their poor behavior. What does that teach them? It teaches them to double down. You have to preemptively reward the good moments. You always look for chances for you to connect and for them to succeed.

You prepare a beautiful bowl of creamy yogurt and plump berries for your older child, and you see your younger one eyeing the display.

Without saying anything, you pour the younger child a glass of milk and place it before them. This is about control, you remember, and so don't make it into a power struggle. Just place it there and step away from the beverage.

You feel a heaviness in your stomach as you worry about your younger child going hours without any food in their belly. You start to question yourself.

"Am I being too strict? Don't I just need them to eat *something*? Why is my kid the only kid who won't eat their breakfast? What am I doing wrong?"

Your inner critic is working on overdrive.

Your younger child takes a long sip of the milk, and you clock it, silently. You're just observing, without interjecting or even editorializing. You're not thinking about what this means, if this will help their morning or behavior, if this is an improvement, or anything; you simply note what is going on objectively.

You take a nonjudgmental stance.

You replace your previous questions with clear statements. Instead of asking if you're being too strict, you reframe it into "I am concerned that by only offering these three choices, I will be negatively impacting my child's day."

Instead of wondering if you should acquiesce, you remind yourself that this is just one meal, on one morning. They are old enough to communicate their needs.

Instead of worrying that you're the only parent who has trouble getting her kids to eat, you say, "I am sure I am not the only person whose children challenge them, and though I wish it were easier, I know that what happens in other families has nothing to do with my family. I cannot control every single thing about my kids, nor should I, and so I need to focus on what I can control, which is keeping my kids safe, focusing on their general well-being, and getting out the door."

You could extrapolate about the future short-term and long-term, but you stay rooted in the moment. You remind yourself to be present, to give yourself grace, to remember that this is just one meal. Will this one meal matter in five minutes? Maybe. In five days? I doubt it. In five years? Absolutely, positively not.

"Ummmm, can I tell you something?" your younger child has come over to you interrupting your coaching session. Your little one looks adorable with a milk mustache, and you see that the glass has been emptied.

"It turns out," your younger child looks at you earnestly. "Blackbeard may not actually be mushy intolerant after all."

Congratulations! You've Collected Coping Mechanism Badge of *Acceptance Ally*.

Turn to page 88 to return to the story.

BONUS: Make the Perfect Plate

One section for each of three ingredients you need to be your best you.

Protein, carbs, fats? Self-compassion, flexibility, freedom? Who is to say? Oh, that's right; you are.

Chapter 6: Romanticizing the Mundane

A Support Story

You steady yourself in the mirror, struggling to recognize your own reflection. There is something simultaneously so familiar and yet so foreign about this ritual, your hands moving effortlessly across jars of lotion, tubes of mascara, stems of brushes. You slick on some lipstick—a soft berry-colored-matte and not the bright coral your BMFF (Best Mom Friend Forever) tried to convince you to don while at the makeup counter last week—and kiss a sticky piece of paper.

You pause your beauty routine to write a note to your kids but have trouble finding the words. It is as if finding the perfect phrasing will guarantee a better day for them; as though with the right message and sealed with a kiss, you can still protect them all day—as though you weren't about to abandon them.

If you're being honest with yourself, which you had to be when you saw your reflection in the department store fluorescent lighting in the aforementioned bright coral lipstick your BMFF tried to convince you to purchase, you aren't abandoning your kids. You're not even lightly leaving them. You're not hurting them. You're not wronging them.

Rather, you're going back to work.

Still, clarifying it doesn't make it feel any easier.

You'd worked before having children, then took a pause when your kids were little, but, now that they are old enough to be in grade school, the time felt right—and also, not right. But it felt more right than not right. Maybe? You know how endlessly lucky you are to even have this option. And you're lucky to have been able to choose to stay home as you had.

You finish writing the note, finish dressing, and try to remember to breathe.

"Now I know how my kids felt on their first day of school," you think to yourself, a pang extending from your heart to your stomach and then back up to your throat.

When you took this new job, you knew that there would be a learning curve, and that almost everything in your life would have to be recalibrated. When discussing your hours with your new employer, you asked for just one thing: a start-time that would allow you to drop your kids off at school. You wanted to be the one to see them off, kiss them goodbye, and tell them how much you love them. And your new boss obliged.

"I cannot believe you *want* to drive carpool," your BMFF had said when you told her the plan.

"Awww, but I love watching them run away with their little backpacks filled with little school supplies . . . with their cute little legs . . ." Your voice had taken on a dreamy quality, suddenly romanticizing all of the mundane parts of motherhood that you'd taken for granted during all of those years home. Now, everything seems precious, a memory not to be missed.

"You're something else," she'd chuckled. "Can I tell you something wild? I actually feel guilty for NOT feeling guilty! I WANT to work! I love working! And I feel bad for that. Imagine that, feeling guilty about guilt. I'm a guilt over-achiever! And who says we can't do it all?" she had joked.

But you had stuck to your carefully constructed plan and are now ready to take your kids to school, before taking yourself to your first day of work. You rack your brain to try to conjure any last-minute tasks. All lunches are packed, the list of emergency contacts is displayed prominently, and you drew a little star next to "orthodontist appointment" on the whiteboard you'd fixed to the fridge, just for emphasis. You're taking any sense of control you can muster.

You wrangle your kids, soaking in every last moment of them. For a long time, you've been relieved to get them out of the house. Now, you feel desperate to stay all together, in a little cocoon of sorts. You long to be close to them, missing them even before you've left.

You make it to school at 8:55 a.m. with five whole minutes to spare. Huge win! It feels fortuitous. You're doing it! This is your day!

This is especially important, as it means you will be able to use the carline system to drop the kids off, as opposed to having to walk them in, sign them in as "tardy" and, importantly, make it to work by the agreed upon time. You don't ever want to be late, but you really don't want to be late today, on day one.

You pull your car up in the loop at the front of the school, eager for one of the teachers to come pluck them from the car, when your kids begin to protest.

"NO! I'm going to miss you!"

"NO! I need you! Can you walk me in?"

"DON'T LEAVE US!"

And you want to crawl under your seat. All you needed was a normal day. Not easy. Not perfect. Not even better than yesterday. Just. Normal. No surprises, no hiccups, no holdups.

"It's Mommy's Law," you hear BMFF's voice in your head, her throaty chuckle echoing. She'd long-ago invented the term to describe the phenomenon of Murphy's Law when anything that can go wrong will go wrong, but applied to parents.

You stare into the rearview mirror and take in the sight of your kids' faces.

You know what to do.

CHOICE POINT: DO YOU USE CARLINE OR WALK THE KIDS IN?

CHOICE 1: If choose to keep the plan and use carline to do a swift, intentional drop-off, turn to page 93.

CHOICE 2: If you choose to park and walk the kids in, turn to page 97.

CHOICE 1: You drop your kids off in carline.

You suddenly feel shaky, which you're sure is a mixture of adrenaline and nerves. You know that to keep the kids calm, you need to stay calm. And so, you plan to validate the kids' feelings but also set firm boundaries.

"I love you, kids. And I'm going to schedule one more minute for you to cry, then I'm going to pull up and let Mrs. H. get you out of the car. Look! She has her whistle around her neck, today! Maybe she will blow it for you!"

They don't oblige, but you know they don't have a choice. You know you're doing the right thing for this moment, but that doesn't make it easier.

You try to mentally coach yourself through their last minute of sobbing. To be your *own* BMFF, you remind yourself of the trust you've built with your kids. You understand this whole experience is part of that trust, even when it is hard. For your family, consistency, routine, and modeling of good behavior are all important, and you know they will serve you well.

Long ago, you'd decided to always say goodbye to your kids when leaving them, reassuring them that you'd always return. Though sneaking out of the room when their backs were turned seemed tempting and easier in the moments, it wasn't your thing. It didn't feel right. You wanted them to know that they *could* turn their backs confidently, knowing that you'd never sneak out and that you *would* be back, because you always would be. You'd learned that a quick sendoff is best, and though it may lead to a few moments of upset, the kids will rally quickly and settle into the comfort of knowing what to expect.

You are true to your word, giving your teary kids a minute, pulling up to the front of the line, and unlocking the doors.

"Good morning, Mrs. H! Please take good care of my little loves today!" You feign cheeriness. You're trying, desperately, to fake it, hoping to, eventually, make it.

"Of course! I always do!" The kind teacher smiles at you, opens the door, and plucks the kids out gently. "Who wants to hear my whistle!?" As the kids leave the car, both in tears, you feel the armor you've been donning start to fall.

Your heart breaks in two.

You make it out of the parking lot before you have to pull over on the side of the road, as the tears have started to flow so forcefully that the road was blurry in front of you. You feel physically sick with guilt.

"What am I doing? What kind of parent am I?" you ask yourself, losing all sense of composure.

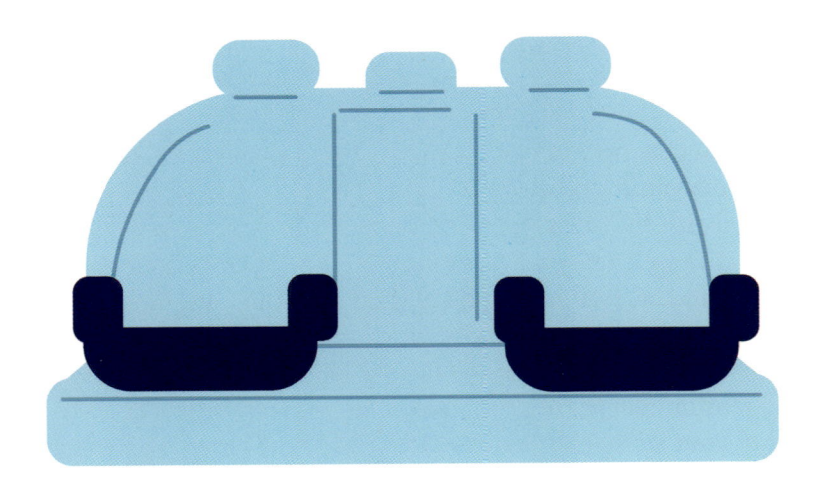

Once again, BMFF's voice appears. She can coach you, even when you can't coach yourself: "You're taking your kids to school and going to work. You're a fantastic mother. You're showing them that they can trust you. You're showing them the value of working hard. You're showing them that you're their parent *and* a human being. Those are all good things."

You know that this is the exact advice you'd be giving to her as well—to any parent, really—it's just so much harder when you have to think about it yourself.

You take a peek at your reflection in the mirror and see all of the carefully applied mascara now streaking down your cheeks. You let out a big exhale. You look out the car window, desperate for a distraction, and, fortuitously, you notice that you've parked under a tree with a canopy of bright red leaves. You can't help but to marvel at their color, as they literally look like the tree has caught fire, The words come to you like magic: leaves on a stream.

You don't remember where you'd learned it, but you'd been taught this exercise long ago, but had not yet had a great excuse to practice it. You turn off your car's motor and shift in your seat until you find a comfortable position.

You close your eyes and visualize a beautiful, moving stream. You try your best to conjure the image as vividly as you can. You take note of its grayish, blueish water and the rocks that poke out from below. You hear the rush of the water as it laps against the grassy shore. You allow yourself to feel your guilt. You welcome each of your intrusive thoughts of guilt and worry, and, as you do, you place each one, mentally, on a leaf that flows down the stream.

As the stream carries the leaves away, you begin to feel the tension easing. You feel a small release in your jaw and the pit in your stomach starts to diminish. After several minutes of doing this visualization exercise, your nervous system has calmed, which allows you to think more clearly and rationally.

You look at the clock, see that school has started for your kids and know that your kids have almost certainly stopped crying. They're in circle time or at their desks and now it's time for your day to begin as well.

You remind yourself to access this feeling of calm every time you need some grounding, today. When you need a reminder, you'll find a window and look out at the vibrant leaves. You've got this. You put on another coat of lipstick, a good song from your playlist, and your first-day-of-work hat. Well, metaphorically, at least for the latter, as you don't yet know the office policy on headwear. And the thought makes you laugh.

It feels good to laugh. And though you might not feel happy all day, you've felt happy for a moment of the day, and that is something you can hold onto.

You turn on your engine, get back onto the road, and head off, ready to re-write Mommy's Law for all.

Congratulations! You've Collected Coping Mechanism Badge Flow Facilitator.

Turn to page 102 to return to the story.

CHOICE 2: You walk your kids into school.

"Okay, guys. I'm going to pull up now and let Mrs. H. get you out of the car. Look! She has her whistle around her neck today! Maybe she will blow it for you!"

They don't oblige, their wailing growing louder.

You know you're doing the right thing for this moment, but that doesn't make it easier. You try to coach yourself through the situation. To be your own BMFF, you remind yourself that they know they can trust you and rely on you. And you know that they know that they need to go to school. But today is an odd day. Maybe, just for today, you'll acknowledge that it's an unusual schedule for all, and extraordinary circumstances can call for some flexibility. You decide that you'll quickly walk them in, reasoning that maybe you all need a softer landing. You've given them the gift of consistency; flexibility can be equally as salient.

"Okay, guys. You are going to school and I am going to work, but, because it is my first day and I know this is a big change, I will park and walk you in. This won't happen again tomorrow, or the next day, but it's just for today while we all get situated.

"So, now we have to finish up with our tears. You are going and so am I, but then I will be back to pick you up! And give you the biggest squeezes!"

This generous announcement is not the antidote you'd hoped. It is going to be a rough, chaotic drop-off. You need to accept it. You can only control so much. You pull your car out of the car line and put your blinker on, signaling the other drivers that you're waiting to park.

But the car in front of you does not move. You don't want to honk—that would feel too yucky—but you only have two minutes. You start to yell at no one in particular, and, really, at everyone in particular.

"MOVE!!" you yell at the driver who most certainly cannot hear you.

"QUIET!!" you yell at your kids, who most certainly can.

The offensive vehicle begins to move, but it's too late. You spot Mrs. H.—whistle and all—turning the carline sign around. In an instant, it goes from "Welcome! Please pull up here!" to "Sorry you're late. Please check in at the office."

You're now tardy, the one thing you'd been so hopeful you'd avoid. The process of getting the kids and their bags and their attitudes and your attitude out of the car and into the building proves tiresome and long. There is whining and crying and begging, and you don't know where yours ends and theirs begins.

It's a chaotic sendoff, the very last thing you wanted on this very important morning. You will be wearing the yucky feelings from this all day, and it will most certainly be more jarring than the coral lipstick would have been.

You give your weepy kids hasty kisses goodbye, not the gentle, compassionate, loving way you'd intended to leave them on this momentous morning. As you get back into your car, you feel the armor you've been donning start to fall.

Your heart breaks in two.

You make it out of the parking lot before you have to pull over on the side of the road, as the tears have started to flow so forcefully that the road was blurry in front of you. You feel physically sick with guilt.

"What am I doing? What kind of parent am I?" you ask yourself, losing all sense of composure.

Once again, BMFF's voice appears. She can coach you,

even when you can't coach yourself: "You're taking your kids to school and going to work. You're a fantastic mother. You're showing them that they can trust you. You're showing them the value of working hard. You're showing them that you're their parent *and* a human being. Those are all good things."

You know that this is the exact advice you'd be giving to her as well—to any parent, really—it's just so much harder when you have to think about it yourself.

So, you call for reinforcements.

BMFF picks up on the first ring, knowing that a call, as opposed to a text, could signal a dire situation. In fact, BMFF doesn't even say "Hello" but rather asks, "What's wrong?" upon answering.

You vent to her, and she listens quietly. You need to get it out, and she understands that. After all, you're her BMFF; she's been there too.

When she does speak, she asks a question you've practiced with one another many times over the years:

"Do you want my advice, or did you need to just vent?" Her tone is kind and loving.

"What have you got for me?" you reply, still feeling sick to your stomach.

"Let me remind you of something you taught me. I'm going to coach you through this. I learned from the best, remember."

You can hear her smile through the phone. "This too shall pass. Remember that. You've gotten through every other hard time that you've faced, thus far. Like, 100 percent of them. Right?"

The sting of the morning's chaos and embarrassment will cause those yucky, guilty feelings for a few minutes. Maybe even an hour. But she's right. You know it will pass

"Now, what number are you?" asks BMFF.

"Um . . . I am about a six," you muster, still a bit shaken.

"Ok, then open up your list and read seven things to me."

"Do you really want me to read them to you?" you are suddenly feeling sheepish.

"Read 'em and please don't weep."

"You're on a roll today," you start. It feels good to smile. You open your phone to the "My Good Things" file in the little notepad app.

Over the years, you and BMFF have developed a system based on a highly scientific mathematical equation:

First, you rate your level of upset on a scale of 1–10.

Then, you take that number, add one to it, and list that number of things that you can do that make you happy. Little things. Things you can control. Things that serve as distractions. Things that engender a genuine sense of pride.

"Ok," you take a deep breath and scan your long list.

"Here goes: 1. I promise to sit outside and let the sun hit my face for at least five minutes during lunch.

2. "I will make myself a cup of coffee with real milk and real sugar.

3. "When I get home, I'll write a few thank you notes and take a walk to the mailbox to send them.

4. "I'll order Thai takeout for dinner, even if no one else wants it.

5. "I will have a two-minute dance party in the kitchen before starting any chores this evening.

6. "I'll play that song, you know the one.

7. "After all of those things I am opening up my computer and treating myself to a nice, fancy, soft new pair of pajamas. Because . . . you know.

"How's that?"

But you don't need BMFF to answer. You already know it for yourself. BMFF just got you there. That is what BMFFs are for, after all.

"You're a pro!" she confirms.

You hang up and open the music app on your phone. And you play that song. You know the one. And as the music swells, your worries begin to fade. As you drive to your first day of work, bopping your head to the music, you start to formulate your dinner order in your head. Why? Because you can.

Congratulations! You've Collected Coping Mechanism Badge of Distress Dossier.

Turn to page 102 to return to the story.

BONUS: The Magic Mental Math Formula

Step 1: Rate your distress on a scale of 1–10.
Step 2: Add 1 to that number.
Step 3: Do that number of things from your distress tolerance activities list.

My List:

-
-
-
-
-
-
-
-
-
-
-

How do you feel now? Better? I knew it!

103

Let's Rap

There are all different ways to cope in stressful situations (duh, you already know this), but one of the ways is to turn the things you want to say into a song. But, what is more fun than a song for a parent who is at her wit's end and just trying to survive?

Why, a rap song, of course!

So, here's your chance to do something ridiculous, outrageous, silly, and, believe it or not, soothing. Who knew rap music could be so soothing!

_____'s Rap Song.
Hi! I am a rapper. My rapper name is
_____
(adjective to denote size) (last thing I ate)
Lil Almonds

Since you've so recently been made aware of your preternatural rapping abilities, let me walk you through your first rap song:

I am _____
But you can call me mom,
And I was busy doing _____
When I just slipped into this rap song.
Today has been _____
And you know what I'm saying,
Cause when it comes to _____
This mom is not playing.
I've already said _____
_____ times,

Can't always go with the flow
Except the flow of my rhymes.
Sometimes I slip, it's hard to get a grip
And the situation with

_____

_____

Is really just the tip
Of the iceberg,
Like it when I rhyme words?
How about _____
_____

See, there's a lot you don't know about me,
I'm a professional _____
At parenting.
What rhymes with stretch marks?

Dance It Out

Instructions: Refer to your Dance-it-Out playlist* and turn the volume up before pressing PLAY. Press PLAY.

*You don't yet have a Dance-it-Out playlist?

Step 1: Fill in the blanks below with the songs that you cannot help but dance to when they are on. Bonus points for songs that also include impassioned lip-syncing. Ex: "I Will Survive"

My Dance-it-Out Playlist:

-
-
-
-
-
-
-
-
-
-
-

Step 2: Now, open whatever device you use to play music. Set up said playlist.

Step 3: Play your Dance-it-Out Playlist. DANCE! SING! Move your body with reckless abandon!

A PORTRAIT OF MY OWN LIFE

Draw a picture of your village. What does it look like? Who is part of it? How does it make you feel? If you have more than one village, that's okay too! More is more, when it comes to villages.

THE TWEEN/ TEEN STORIES

In which we discuss:
Self-Respect
Wise Mind
Rupture & Repair

Chapter 7: I Can't Stop It from Raining, but I Can Give You an Umbrella

A Self-Respect Story

It is a gray morning and only continuing to darken. Opaque clouds hang low as they begin to pummel the peaceful, dove-colored sky.

It is stormy: the kind of storm that shakes the house and sways the trees.

Everything feels harder on rainy days, and you don't know why. Is it because we don't operate as well without light? Is it just a formed habit? It's hard to determine which has come first, the chicken or the egg, or the storm or a tough morning, as it were.

It is a quarter to twelve, five minutes before your last virtual meeting of the morning will end so that you can finally sit down for a meal. It will be your first of the day, which you know isn't good, but you haven't had a second to yourself. You scribble "meal prep" on a Post-it and stick it to the top of your computer and your stomach growls loudly.

Thank goodness you're on mute.

You've taken to writing little notes to yourself, as it's one way to prevent the little things from slipping through the cracks. Everyone tells you to use your phone or your robot, but you are faithfully old school. You still use a planner and you still use Post-it notes, and you still forget things, but far less than you would without these tools.

You hear another rumble, and you're not sure if it is the weather or your hungry stomach once again. Images of neat rows of mason jars, neatly organized and filled with layers of produce and grains, begin to fill your head. This is what hunger does to you.

When the meeting ends, you hold yourself back from clapping. You're so grateful for this respite. It's been a hard time at work, and you feel constantly torn between your obligations there and your obligations at home. You're like the most elegantly dressed, well-educated wishbone that there ever was. Wishbone. Chicken. You are still so hungry.

You turn off your camera, open the fridge, and start to scan the shelves when your phone rings. You assume it's one of your colleagues, hoping to debrief with you, and so you expect to screen it (that leftover taco salad is calling your name!!!), but, when you look down, you realize your mistake.

You see a familiar number flash on the screen. You look down and see, with the feeling of dread only elicited by such a sight, that the call is coming from your child's middle school. Instantly, your appetite disappears

Without even bothering to close the refrigerator door, you pick up. You spit out the words, "Is-everything-okay?" as if they're one long multihyphenate.

"Hi, there," says a cheery voice on the other end. "It's not an emergency. Everything is fine. We are calling from the school nurse's office, as your child has asked to speak with you."

You exhale. You didn't realize that you'd been holding your breath. You listen carefully as the nurse explains that your tween has come in twice, so far, this morning, complaining of "not feeling well."

You are relieved and not relieved. On one hand, everything is fine. That is always great news—the most important news, of course. On the other hand, it is not something clear cut. You remember the days when your tween, then a younger kid, would call with acute I-want-parent-itis presenting as a terrible malady that, astonishingly, would disappear the moment they got into your car. The best was when your child, then in second grade, complained of blurriness and headaches, and when they were given a vision screening in the school nurse's office, they claimed they could only read the little letters, but not the larger ones.

It's much better now as your kid can communicate, both expressively and receptively, but still.

You know that, no matter what, this decision is going to be your call. As much as you hate to admit it, a fever or positive strep test, though miserable, is easier than this gray area. The school will leave it up to you and it's not something you'd planned for.

"Hello?" you hear your child's quivering voice and your heart, once again, sinks into your feet.

"What's going on?" you ask, rhetorically. Open-ended questions are not always the right move with this kid, but in this case, with these variables, it is important that, regardless of what happens, your tween feels heard.

"I don't know, I am just feeling really bad. I'm having a terrible day. I need to go home."

"What kind of bad?" you ask. "I want to remind you that you can . . . you *need* to be honest with me. I take physical and mental health issues just as seriously, but I need to know."

"A little physically bad. Like, a tiny bit. My head hurts and my stomach has been upset all morning. But very emotionally yucky."

"Thank you for being honest," you praise your child for their transparency, in not so many words. "You will be okay."

You reassure them, despite having no idea what dragon will need slaying. The most important thing is to emphasize that, no matter what, they will be okay. They are strong. They are resilient. They can do hard things.

Then, the nurse pipes in. "You know," she begins, her tone notably less warm than it had been just a moment ago, "we've had to call you *several* times this year, so far. We wouldn't want anyone taking advantage, would we?"

You are instantly put-off by her tone and implication.

You could get angry, be rude, or even allow her judgments to impact your decision. If you're trying to model empowerment, however, you can't let those things happen. You already feel guilty enough, wondering what kind of parent this makes you. You're the wishbone, being pulled, once again.

You stick to your family's mantra, repeating it to the nurse; for the nurse: "In our family, we treat physical and mental health equally, and so I trust my child to tell me what's going on."

You feel shakier than you sound.

"Okay, then," she replies. Truthfully, the nurse has no choice, though you, in some ways, envy her position. You wish you didn't have a choice, either. But you do, and you weigh your options. How do you decide what to do? There is no right answer; there is no wrong answer. Whatever you choose, the most important thing is how you are able to communicate in this moment.

"May I speak to my child, again, please?"

CHOICE POINT: DO YOU LEAVE YOUR CHILD AT SCHOOL OR DO YOU PICK THEM UP?

CHOICE 1: If you agree to pick your child up from school, turn to page 112.

CHOICE 2: If you decide that today, for whatever reason feels right in this moment (or, at least, the most right), you will not be picking your child up from school, turn to page 117.

CHOICE 1: You pick up your child.

"Hey, kiddo. I really appreciate you opening up to me," you explain.

You take a moment to collect yourself, repeating your words just to buy some time.

You've been here before. As the nurse made sure to remind you, you've received a call from her office more times than you can remember for more things than you'd care to remember. But you know that you need to show respect, both to your child and, importantly, to yourself.

You look up at the Post-it where you've written all of your important acronyms. Being a parent is a journey, and you've learned that visual cues are really helpful for you. It's easy to know something intellectually, but much harder to apply it, especially when emotions are involved. You scan many combinations of letters until you land on the right four. You've neatly written the letters *F.A.S.T.* with "for self-respect" scrawled underneath.

F.A.S.T.
fair   apologies   stick to values   truthful

Communication is one of your family's greatest values, and acting in accordance with your values means a lot. In order to achieve the most comfortable outcome for yourself, while communicating effectively to your child, you start to go through the letters in the acronym. *F* is for fair; *A* for apologies; *S* for stick to values, and *T* for truthful.

You thank your past self for preparing you for this moment, allowing you to check your own feelings of self-respect in any situation, so that you can ward off the guilt before it even has a chance to creep in.

F: Be fair, not only to others but to yourself.

A: Don't apologize unless it is really warranted. You don't need to apologize for making the decision that you feel is best.

S: Stick to your values. Honesty is one of your top values, and so it should be rewarded and reinforced.

T: Be truthful. Always this.

"I am really proud of you," you continue. "That was really brave."

"I need a mental health day," your child interrupts.

"I know that you are able to do really hard things," you encourage.

As you prepare to continue, you remind yourself to be clear and direct. If you do not verbalize this next message confidently, you could be laying the groundwork for an undesirable habit. You can't always avoid those things, so you remind yourself not to be too hard on yourself. You, too, can do hard things. And setting ourselves up for success is always preferable. Just the fact that you are trying should count for something.

You have this next part down, like a script that you've been rehearsing in your head without realizing it: muscle memory, perhaps. Your child needs to know that you are there when they need you and that they are also able to be there for themself. They must learn to differentiate between *want* and *need*.

"Right now, I am going to come get you. You were honest, shared a hard thing about your mental health, and made it clear that this feels important. But I want to be clear with you, kiddo. If I chose not to pick you up today, you'd still be okay. In this moment, you feel safe and are safe. I want to reassure you of that. And I want to remind you that if you call me, again, tomorrow, as long as you are healthy and safe, I am not going to pick you up again. This is reserved for the times when you really need it—not for times like your ear aches at camp when you didn't want to swim . . ."

"Thanks for listening to me. I love you," your tween interrupts, seemingly desperate for you to not bring up the summer when he feigned swimmer's ear to avoid the deep end.

You continue, "I'll be there in ten minutes. Make sure you get all of your work from each of your teachers. This isn't a video-games day. You can curl up with a book or finish your homework. I still need to have lunch, and I have a few meetings this afternoon, but afterwards we can cuddle or have chai or chat. And, I have another idea for us to try. I will see you soon."

Your monologue is over, and you nailed it! Applause rings (in your head) and a standing ovation erupts (in your head). You take a bow and head towards the door. You don't feel great about this outcome, but you can cope with your uncomfortable feelings. They will, as always, pass. You've done some heavy lifting, already. You grab a protein bar on your way out the door to tide you over. Lunch will have to wait a little longer.

You know that when your tween gets home, you will do your best to get them to open up, knowing that you may or may not be successful. Staying connected at this stage is challenging yet crucial. But you will continue to do your best to empower them. After you are done with your work, you have a plan for the two of you. Together, you'll work on a sensory kit, one that they can bring with them in their school bag, so that next time they're feeling anxious or bummy or blue at school, they have a tangible tool.

You actually made one for yourself years ago, and it helps you when you are traveling or before big meetings or on those gloomy, gray days when everything really does seem a bit harder.

You will instruct your tween to find things that bring them calm, using their senses. You'll talk about ideas: a bottle of lavender essential oil to smell, a mint tea bag, a family photo, a piece of dark chocolate, a soft keychain that you've always rubbed for luck.

Having tools—both ones you can hold physically and ones you can hold close to your heart—reminds you of your power, and you'll keep working to fill your toolbox too.

You've repeated a phrase to your tween since they were a little kid, and it feels particularly apt in this moment: "I can't stop it from raining, but I can give you an umbrella."

And that is exactly what you'll do.

Congratulations! You've Collected Coping Mechanism Badge of *F.A.S.T. Friend*.

Turn to page 121 to return to the story.

CHOICE 2: You do *not* pick up your child.

"I really appreciate you opening up to me," you explain.

You take a moment to collect yourself, repeating your words just to buy some time.

You've been here before. As the nurse made sure to remind you, you've received a call from her office more times than you can remember for more things than you'd care to remember. But you know that you need to show respect, both to your child and, importantly, to yourself.

You look up at the note where you've written all of your important acronyms. Being a parent is a journey, and you've learned that visual cues are really helpful tools for you. It's easy to know something intellectually, but much harder to apply it, especially when emotions are involved. You scan many combinations of letters until you land on the right four. You've neatly written the letters *G.I.V.E* with "for positive communication (e.g., avoid fighting!!!!)" scrawled underneath.

Communication is one of your family's greatest values, and acting in accordance with your values means a lot. In order to achieve the most comfortable outcome for yourself, while communicating effectively to your child, you start to go through the letters in the acronym: *G* is for gentle; *I* for interested; *V* for validate; and *E* for easy manner.

How do those words apply? *G.I.V.E.* is a way to encourage healthy communication in relationships, so that you can ward off the guilt before it even has a chance to creep in.

G: No attacks, no judging, lead with kindness, be *gentle*.

I: Make sure the other person feels heard, be genuinely *interested*.

V: *Validate* the person's feelings and fears.

E: Use an *easy*, warm tone of voice.

"I am really proud of you," you continue. "That was really brave. You are a brave kid. You can do hard things."

"I need a mental health day," your child interrupts.

"I want you to think carefully about this. Do you *need* a mental health day, or do you *want* a mental health day?"

Your tween takes a beat before answering your question, as you expected they would.

"Well . . . this isn't the worst I've ever felt . . ."

This gives you the context you needed. You remind yourself to be clear and direct. If you verbalize this next line in the form of a question, you'll be stuck. If you ask your kid if they can handle staying in school, they will likely decline. So, you tell them the plan. You show the immense confidence you have in that awesome kid of yours. That's what parents do, after all.

"I can't see you right now, but your voice sounds pretty calm. What color are you?"

You refer to the Zones of Regulation you and your family have practiced since your tween was a tantrumming toddler: four colors—green, blue, yellow, red—to denote the severity of the level of distress at any moment. Tools are hard to access in the red zone, so, if possible, we have tried to catch ourselves before getting to that point.

"Yellow," they reply.

"Okay, thank you for telling me. I hear you. And knowing what I know about how you are feeling, I am going to have you stay at school today and get back to class. I know you don't want to do this, but I also know that you can use your tools. This way, you get to play ultimate frisbee after school today. I know you don't want to miss that, right?"

They hum an affirmative.

"I love you so much and I am so proud of you."

Quick, clear, painless. Well, not painless, but bearable.

"But wait," your child sounds pained.

You ache. The thought of them in pain is like a dagger in your chest. But you know that both feelings, yours and theirs, will pass. So, you swoop right back in, with a script that you've been rehearsing in your head without realizing it: muscle memory, perhaps. Your child needs to know that you are there when they need you and that they are also able to be there for themself. You continue.

"You were honest, shared a hard thing about your mental health, and made it clear that this feels important. I want to reassure you that I hear you. And that you've got this. I know it. Because you're you. This is not like your ear aches at camp when you didn't want to swim . . ."

"'K, love you, bye!" Your tween interrupts, seemingly desperate for you to not bring up the summer when they feigned swimmer's ear to avoid the deep end.

You hear a click and then a dial tone.

They've hung up and, presumably, gone back to class. You nailed it. Applause rings (in your head) and a standing ovation erupts (in your head). Sort of. In your gut, it doesn't feel so great, but it feels *right*. Right is often different than easy. You give a hard swallow, imagine yourself taking a bow, and scribble the word *resilience* on the notepad in front of you.

It's taco salad time.

Congratulations! You've Collected Coping Mechanism Badge of *G.I.V.E. Guru.*

Turn to page 121 to return to the story.

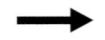

BONUS: Zones of Regulation Worksheet

Today I feel:

Today I look:

Today my color is:

Use this template or create your own tool, using symbols and colors that represent each zone.

The colors you choose are up to you, as we all see the world differently. However, for many people, the color green signifies happiness or peace, the color blue represents feeling sad or tired, the color yellow represents feeling anxious or excited and red signifies anger or panic.

As we move from zone to zone, we will notice changes in our bodies and minds and can use different skills to cope.

Build Your Own Sensory Kit

In my kit, I will include:
_____ to smell
_____ to see
_____ to hear
_____ to touch
_____ to taste

Chapter 8: Your Carbon Footprint!?

A Wise Mind Story

"Ouch!" You instinctively put your half-open mouth on your forearm, right where the hot oil had just splattered.

"Why do we do that?" You wonder to yourself as you turn on the kitchen faucet and put your arm under the cool water, deciding that was a better move than your arm-to-mouth reflex.

A small drop of hot oil will not dampen your excitement: You've created a masterpiece and have never been prouder. Culinarily proud, that is. You smile as you picture your family members' reactions. Though this will be a special dinner for everyone, this meal is especially for your teen. Now that they are an official teenager, you've found it harder to find things you two can connect on. It's a phase you weren't ready for, and so you don't quite know how to cope. Or, that is, you didn't: enter cooking!

You've done it! You've turned the problem on its head as you've recreated your teen's favorite meal on earth. Not only is it their absolute favorite meal ever, but it is attached to one of your most cherished family memories. You will never forget the look on your teen's face when they were presented with their brimming bowl on your best-ever family vacation. You've never seen that child eat with such gusto, and it has since been the subject of fodder and fantasy.

And, after all this time, you had the brilliant idea of recreating this dish, now infused with the essence of connection and your abundant love. You are certain that your teen will not only be surprised, but they will also be thrilled. Clear eyes. Full bellies. Can't lose.

You've been working for days on this feast: from shopping at three different stores for just the right ingredients (meat must be 80 percent lean and absolutely not 85 percent; red wine vinegar must be a Lambrusco and nothing else), to hand rolling dough, to using a mandolin to slice vegetables when you'd previously been certain that a mandolin was an instrument that made sound and not very thinly sliced produce. It's a labor of love, and you've never enjoyed any type of labor more, though even the word conjures images of your teen as a tiny, perfect baby, and your eyes fill with tears.

You set the table, check the stove, and taste test every bite, savoring every last drop in a way that many would find gross, but you really don't care. You twist the pepper grinder and tear basil as though you're in your own cooking show.

You allow your mind to wander back to that family vacation and its magic. You're certain you're probably glossing over some of the realities, like lost luggage and sibling spats, but you'll never forget the sense of togetherness your family felt that summer. It felt like it was your family against the world in a way that created bonds and made memories. You hadn't seen your teen that happy in a long time, and so your excitement about being able to recreate that experience is palpable. You've even had the idea of taking a new family picture, similar to the photo from that trip. In the original, your teen had been holding up their plate, eyes wide, smile so broad it was goofy, and you've held that image like a snapshot in your mind ever since. It was . . . is . . . the most endearing portrait. You wear your longing to reconnect like a favorite sweater.

When you call your family in for dinner, each person who walks in comments on the smell. It smells amazing. When you present the meal, their eyes grow wide, just like you'd hoped. The presentation. The aroma. You want to tell your teen that you've done this especially for them, but you are confident that they'll just know. You take great care in serving each person, feeling satisfied and thrilled. You save your teen for last, as their approval is really the approval you're after. You take one last moment to fantasize about how this will go.

Maybe they will offer to help me with the dishes and we will get into a soapy, sudsy water fight, just like we did when they were little!

Maybe they will be so stuffed that they will simply snuggle up to me on the couch, resting their head on my shoulder. It's been so long since they've done that.

As you go to serve them, your anticipation growing, your teen crosses their hands over the plate, back and forth.

When did their hands get so big? Are they adding to the flair? Are they telling you to load it up?

It doesn't compute.

"None for me, thanks." Their voice has changed since this morning, sounding even more mature.

You laugh and continue to hover over their plate.
Very funny! My teenager is charming me already!

"Seriously. I am not eating meat right now. I'm trying to decrease my carbon footprint, remember? I told you this last week."

And then, in one fluid motion, you see your dreams and hopes come crashing down around you, when . . .

They. Roll. Their. Eyes. At. You.

At first, you are stunned. Food drips from the spoon and onto the cloth tablecloth you'd used just for this occasion, but you don't even notice. In this moment, all of your blood seems to rush to your head, and you truly understand the expression *seeing red* as adrenaline courses through you. This can't be happening. They are rejecting this beautiful dinner that you worked so hard to create. But, more than that, they are rejecting you.

And you can't take it.

CHOICE POINT: HOW DO YOU CHOOSE TO REACT?

CHOICE 1: If you explode, turn to page 127.
CHOICE 2: If you implode, turn to page 133.

CHOICE 1: EXPLOSION!

You let go of the plate, letting it fall and then shatter, spraying its saucy contents all over.

Your head swims.

You hear yourself yelling, but it's muffled, as though you've floated up and out of your body.

"Are you kidding me!? Do you know how hard I worked!? You are rude and selfish, and I am so disappointed in you! Don't you care about any of us anymore?! Don't you care about how we feel? I don't even know you anymore!"

While there are kernels of truth to this, this is a completely hyperbolic, wholly inappropriate reaction. Still, you can't help it. You feel your adrenaline continue to surge, as your fight or flight response has been activated.

You fight.

"Your carbon footprint!? Your CARBON FOOTPRINT?! What about the footprints you're leaving on my heart as you stomp all over it!?"

You're feeling awful, in both the "bad" way and the "regretful" way. How did something so positive turn so quickly? You step over the mess of shattered porcelain and spilled sauce, thinking the scene was the exact physical representation of how you're feeling.

The tears start to fall as you leave the room, stomp into your bathroom, and collapse onto the closed toilet seat. As you sit and sob, you think of all the times you'd been sitting on that very toilet when your child, so small, had barged in and climbed right up onto your lap. No boundaries, no distance, no mercurial carbon footprint.

You give yourself a moment to sit in your feelings, to really, deeply experience them.

You sit that way for a few minutes, head in your hands, heart on the floor, and you realize that giving yourself this permission to feel is actually helping. You think of the "Bear Hunt" song you used to sing with your teen when they were little.

> *We're going on a bear hunt,*
> *We're going to catch a big one, we're not scared!*
> *Uh oh! Tall grass!*

"If only obstacles now were as simple as tall grass," you think to yourself, validating your own feelings of sorrow.

> *We can't go over it,*
> *We can't go under it*
> *We have to go through it!*

"The problem may be different," you continue. "But the solution is not. I can't avoid it. I can't run from it. I need to go through it."

Sorrow washes over you, but you don't stop it. Finally, all of the things you've been fretting over and feeling cascade over your whole being. This change in your dynamic has been hard for you, and you've been mourning something you didn't even fully realize you'd lost.

You give yourself time to be in it—in the woods and the tall grass and the mud of it—and, when you've gotten out many of your tears, you decide to start forging your way out.

To do so, you use your wise mind. You conjure the image of a Venn diagram: on one side, your emotional mind;

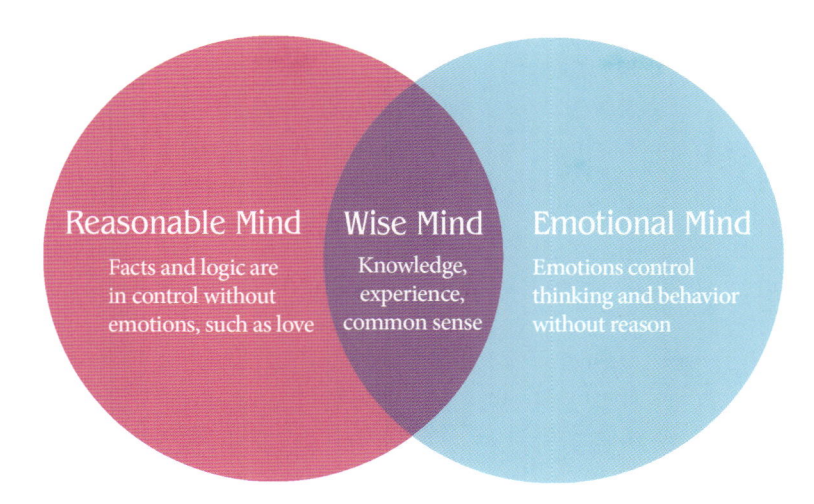

Reasonable Mind
Facts and logic are in control without emotions, such as love

Wise Mind
Knowledge, experience, common sense

Emotional Mind
Emotions control thinking and behavior without reason

on the other, your reasonable mind; and, in the middle, in that little sliver of space where the two minds overlap, you picture your *wise mind*. This space is where the feeling of your *heart* and wisdom of your *head* come together.

It's almost as if one side is the *over it* and the other is the *under it* and you're going to meet in the spot where you can go *through it*.

You think of your emotional mind and, once again, try to name the feelings you're sitting with:

You feel disappointed.
You feel frustrated.
You feel angry.
You feel dejected.
You feel rejected.

You feel scared.

You're scared that you're losing your child and the relationship you once had. Your emotional mind is subjective, temperamental, and ruled by your feelings. You think of your rational mind, that is pragmatic, logical, rational, and static. It is where you problem-solve, plan, and reason. You picture the wise mind and figure out how to make these two hemispheres converge.

The middle path.

The way through. To proceed mindfully you begin to ask yourself the hard questions:

"What are my goals?"

"How can I set us both up for success?"

"What steps can we take to improve the situation?"

As you go through the mental exercises, you notice that your tears have dried up, your breathing has regulated, and your thoughts are no longer racing through your mind. You're regulated.

You hear a soft knock on the door to the bathroom and you smile at the irony of your teen *now* knowing to knock. Then, you wanted space. Now, you want them as close to you as possible. Another middle path to be found.

"You okay?" Your teen's voice sounds familiar, once more.   This is comforting.

"One second," you say, steadying yourself at the sink. You splash some cold water over your face, a trick that has always helped to calm your body when in distress, and wipe your eyes. When you open the door and your teen sees your red eyes, they ask you again.

"You good?" As though they're making sure you're okay. Making sure you're still you. Making sure you're still theirs.

131

Without words, you wrap your arms around them in a hug. They are just so much bigger.

"I'm sorry."

"No, I'm sorry, honey. I should never have reacted like that. I've just been . . ." You remind yourself to be intentional and clear. "I'm trying to adjust to this new stage. You're so much older now, and you need me so much less, and . . . I miss you."

"I haven't gone anywhere. I'm still here," they say. This is the closest you've felt to them in longer than you can remember.

"I know," you sniff, again. "I just miss spending time with you. You don't have to rely on me in the same way anymore. I don't know how to connect with you. I just want to make you happy."

Somehow, in the quiet room, this feels intimate and safe. You're able to say the things that have been too hard to acknowledge, let alone utter out loud.

You're going through it, together.

"Yeah, I'm growing up. I know you're always here for me, I'm just trying to learn to stand on my own. To make my own mistakes."

And they're right. You must accept the reality and stop fighting it. You won't win, and all you're doing is exhausting yourself with a futile exercise that will only serve to make you both miserable. You can't reason your way out, for if you could, dinner would have been perfect. You can't feel your way out, for if you could, you'd not be crying alone in the bathroom. But you can use your wise mind.

You need to accept that your child is growing, just as you've given them the tools to do, and you must be willing to evolve with them. They are growing, no matter how hard you fight the change. And you wouldn't if you could, as, ultimately that's what you want; you wouldn't have it any other way.

Sometimes, you have to hold two things at the same time: You want them to grow, and you can acknowledge that it's hard. So, you resolve to stop fighting it. To tamp the intensity of your feelings. You're going to take control back, but in a way that is appropriate and realistic. You make a plan.

"Hey," you begin, "do you think we could try to take some time after dinner, once a week, to just chat? Even if it's for five minutes? Even if you don't want to talk. We can just take a walk or watch something. Plus, we can leave the dishes for everyone else!"

"That sounds great," your teen replies. You look at your child and see, in their eyes, that they are still the same kid you've always known and loved—just in a slightly different package.

"Come on," you say, motioning to them with a playful smile. "Let's go eat some cereal."

Congratulations! You've Collected Coping Mechanism Badge of Heart & Head Harmony.

Turn to page 138 to return to the story.

CHOICE 2: IMPLOSION!

Your grip on the serving plate begins to slip, as your hands are shaking so fiercely. You place it down on the table, feeling dizzy.

You hear your own voice excusing yourself, but it's muffled, as though you've floated up and out of your body.

The deluge of tears begins before you leave the room.

You're feeling awful, in both the "bad" way and the "regretful" way. How did something so positive turn so quickly? You feel your adrenaline surge as your "fight or flight" response has been activated. You choose to walk out (rather, your amygdala does).

Flight.

You open the door from the kitchen and step outside.

As you stand on your stoop, in the cool, night air, the sound of neighborhood children laughing and playing is as jarring a sound as a siren or storm would be. You're flooded with feelings of wistfulness, which is one of the hardest feelings for you to identify, let alone reconcile.

You let yourself feel your feelings. Sometimes, a good sensorial cue can allow you to dig into those deep emotions. An evocative song, a familiar smell, a reminder of the past in a way that is hard to describe. You stand and feel, until it is time to stop. Not quit, but rather, to use a helpful acronym: *S. T. O. P.*

> *S*: Stop.
> *T*: Take a step back.
> *O*: Observe.
> *P*: Proceed mindfully.

As you breathe in the fresh air, you name your feelings:
You feel disappointed.
You feel frustrated.
You feel angry.
You feel rejected.
You feel scared.

You're scared that you're losing your child and the relationship you once had. You take a step back from the situation. You take some long, deep breaths. You are feeling shaky.

Inhale. Exhale. Inhale. Exhale.

As you focus on your intentional breathing, you take time to observe. You aim to be objective in noticing what is going on inside of you and what is going on around you. Where are you jumping to conclusions and what is more deeply rooted in reality?

To proceed mindfully you begin to ask yourself the hard questions:

"What are my goals?"

"How can I set us both up for success?"

"What steps can we take to improve the situation?"

As you go through the mental exercises, you notice that your breathing has slowed and the shaking has subsided.

You hear a soft knock on the door to the outside and you smile at the irony of someone knocking to get out rather than knocking to get in.

"You okay?" Your teenager's voice sounds familiar, once more.

Without giving them a verbal reply, you wrap your arms around them in a hug. They are so much bigger now.

"I'm sorry."

"No, I'm sorry, honey. I should never have reacted like that. I've just been . . ." You remind yourself to be intentional and clear. "I miss you."

"I haven't gone anywhere. I'm still here," your teen says. This is the closest you've felt to them in longer than you can remember.

"I know," you sniff, again. "I just miss spending time with you. You don't need me in the same way anymore. I don't know how to connect with you. I just want to make you happy."

Somehow, in the fresh evening air, this feels intimate and safe. You're able to say the things that have been too hard to acknowledge, let alone utter out loud.

"Yeah, I'm growing up. I know you're always here for me, I'm just trying to learn to stand on my own. To make my own mistakes."

And they're right. You must accept the reality and stop fighting it. You won't win, and all you're doing is exhausting yourself with a futile exercise that will only serve to make you miserable.

You need to accept that your child is growing, just as you've given them the tools to do, and you must be willing to evolve with them. They will continue growing, no matter how hard you fight the change. And, really, you don't want to fight it; growth is exactly what you want.

Sometimes, you have to hold two things at the same time: you want them to grow *and* you can acknowledge that it's hard. So, you resolve to stop fighting it. To tamp the intensity of your feelings. You're going to take control back, but in a way that is appropriate and realistic. You make a plan.

"Hey," you begin. "Do you think we could try to take a few minutes to swing?"

"What?" Your teen looks puzzled. You can't blame them, as it's been a truly wacky evening.

"Can we just swing a little? You know, on your old play structure. I don't know, when you were little, we used to do it all the time, and sometimes movement helps. I feel like I need to get rid of some nervous energy. Wanna try? Even if it's for five minutes? I don't know . . ." You cut yourself off, worried you've sounded foolish. You can't take any more embarrassment that evening.

"That sounds great," they reply, and look like they mean it. You look at your child, who is evolving more and more into a young adult by the day, and see, in their eyes, that they are still the same kid you've always known and loved, just in a slightly different package.

"Come on," you say, motioning to them, "I'll beat you to high swing."

And, off you go, until it's *your* giggles echoing in the distance of the night, mingling in the air with the happy chants and cheers of children—and the parents who love and yearn for them—everywhere.

Congratulations! You've Collected Coping Mechanism Badge of *S.T.O.P. Star*.

Turn to page 138 to return to the story.

BONUS: Mind Your Wise Mind

Use this blank Wise Mind template in order to mindfully navigate your own moments of distress, discomfort, confusion, or chaos. What is your heart saying? What is your head saying? Where can they meet in the middle? Finding your own version of Wise Mind is about practice and not perfection. The more you practice, the easier this will become. Look at you go!

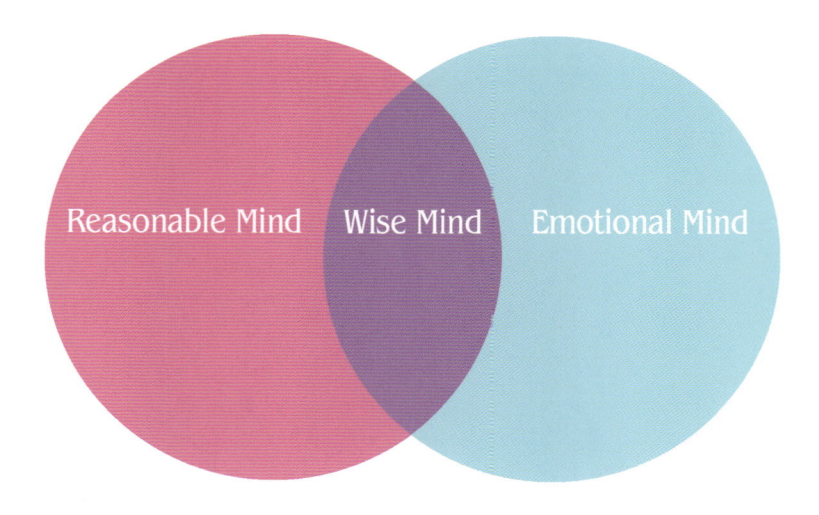

Reasonable Mind   Wise Mind   Emotional Mind

Chapter 9: Flattering and Shattering

A Rupture and Repair Story

As the shower water pounds on you, you begin to relax for the first time in . . . you truly do not know how long. It's been a hard day . . . week? Month? It's been hard.

"Why doesn't anyone talk about how hard it is?" you're always wondering.

Showers are your time to think. You let your mind continue its question spree.

"Everyone I know posts the most perfect photos on social media. Everyone is dressed perfectly (coordinated, obviously), and smiling perfectly, in their perfectly tidy homes with their perfectly Instagrammable lives. Why don't they post the moments when the baby spits up or the teenager comes in an hour after curfew, and you yell at someone for no reason, and life is messy?"

It's a question that has many answers and, also, none.

You take a deep inhale, savoring the scent of lavender that wafts through the steam that's accumulating around you. Aromatics and ideas swirl through the warm, wet air. The water is scalding, just how you like it. Not hot enough to burn you, but the tiniest bit too hot in a way that feels so good. Especially today.

You've reserved this shower time and are coveting each moment.

You've instructed your teenage kids to take care of the dog, set the table, and do their homework, which has, admittedly, gotten lighter as the school year draws to a close. Really, you don't care if they end up on their phones, as long as you get this time to yourself.

And you've secured reinforcements: their other parent. Not that your kids need that kind of support anymore. In some ways, you long for the days when they needed you for everything. In others, you are supremely grateful for their independence and self-sufficiency.

But, as they say, as they've gotten bigger, so have the problems. When they come home from school crying, it isn't just sad "because Alice crushed my paper bird" but, rather, it's gutting because "Alice won't let me sit with her crew at lunch anymore."

The fact that your teenager has taken to spending her weekend nights with you, on the couch, in front of whatever true crime show is on the television is both a testament to your closeness and a reminder of the tenuousness of their friendships. You long for the days when you could just call another parent to set up a playdate. If you're being totally honest, you long for the days when kids had to call their friends at home, on a landline, and say, "Hello, Mr./Mrs./Ms. ____ is my friend ____ there, please?"

But, instead, you can't make those calls, your teen won't make those calls, and, as of late, the other kids don't make those calls to them.

Your new weekend ritual is flattering and shattering.

You're doing your best to trust the universe, the values you've imparted, and the resilience that everyone assures you this time will foster. Well, in this very moment, you're doing your best to clean yourself without your thoughts spiraling. You've just started your first shampoo when the first one creeps in.

"What if they end up with no friends, alone, forever?"

You begin to coach yourself through the mental exercise, trying to evaluate what you can and cannot control, as well as what worrying about the situation will or will not accomplish when you remember:

This shower is your time to relax.

You try again, shaking the shampoo bottle. It's not working, as another thought, insidious and sneaky, creeps in. More than a thought, it's a feeling.

Guilt. Something you know well.

"Why can't they just be like other kids? Why can't they be normal?"

In this moment, you feel crushed, two times over. First, you're gutted by the content of your worries. How painful it is to go there. But, more deeply, you feel awful that you have this thought in the first place.

In all ways, you know, with every ounce of your being, that you'd never trade your kid for anything. That they are perfect exactly how they are. You just wish life weren't so hard for them.

Guilt falls over you with the shower water. The spiral you've been trying to avoid begins to pelt you with feelings of guilt, shame, and worry.

You have spent the day both actively and passively caring for your kids, but you worry you haven't really given them quality time. And so the Googling, planning, chauffeuring, cooking, and such feel less than. It never feels good enough. Not for the kids, necessarily, but for yourself, for your own standards; the impossibly high bar you've set for yourself.

You find it funny (and, by funny, you mean infuriating) when people used to ask if their other parent was babysitting.

People don't ask that parent that question when they go out, go to work, or make travel plans.

"No, they are not babysitting," you'd mastered your reply. "We refer to it as *parenting*."

How can one, small shower contain so many big, woesome thoughts?

You try to rinse the worries from your hair along with your clarifying shampoo, and, just as you're emulsifying the other shampoo on your hands, readying it for your second scrub, the bathroom door flings open. They can't see you, but you brace yourself, nonetheless. The steam evaporates instantly, along with your sense of tranquility.

"Excuse me!" you have to shout to be heard over the pounding water.

"Help! Crosby got into something! We need to use the shower!"

This takes a moment to sink in.

The dog has gotten into something and has, presumably, gotten himself dirty enough that he needs to be hosed down, and so you'll need to vacate the shower so that the dog can be washed?

How is this reality? They were supposed to be watching him! How is it that you can't take ten minutes for yourself without chaos ensuing?

"I'm sorry! I got distracted on my phone, and he was only outside alone for a second . . ." your tween sounds sheepish. As they should.

Next, you hear the voice of your partner emerge.

The bathroom is becoming crowded with bodies and maladies.

"He managed to get into some mud, or at least I hope it's mud," your partner explains.

Not only are you only one-third of the way through your shower, naked, getting colder by the minute, aggravated, and, lest they forget, soaking wet, but there is no single chore you loathe as much as washing the dog.

CHOICE POINT: DO YOU TELL YOUR FAMILY TO LEAVE OR OFFER TO HELP?

CHOICE 1: If you ask them to leave (avoiding chaos), turn to page 144.
CHOICE 2: If you offer to help (accepting chaos), turn to page 148.

CHOICE 1: You avoid the chaos.

You take a beat, as your instinct to hop out and help surfaces.

But, at the same time, you feel deeply resentful of this dynamic.

Why do you have to clean up every mess, literally and figuratively?

Why must you carry the weight of everyone's emotions on your sudsy shoulders?

We can't have an existence where a shower is not just a luxury, but an actual possibility.

You lean into your feelings and think about the parenting technique you've been practicing since your children were little: *Nurtured Heart*. The two words have always resonated with you. It's a loving concept that promotes healthy boundaries. You remind yourself of the three pillars of this approach that have worked so well for you and your family: Be absolutely clear, absolutely find joy in each moment, and absolutely do not add to the chaos. Children of all ages are really just craving connection.

You muster up your courage and proceed.

"I can't help with Crosby right now," you begin.

Immediately, you feel guilty. This is hard. You're prioritizing yourself at this moment and it feels foreign and yucky.

"But, wait . . ." your teen starts.

"I don't think this can wait," your partner finishes.

Be absolutely clear, you tell yourself.

"Then you can take him outside and use the hose to clean him off."

"Uh . . . okay . . ." you hear your teen's voice waver a bit, a departure from their characteristic coolness.

Absolutely find joy in this moment, you tell yourself.

"Maybe, when you finish, you can have an old-school water fight," you suggest. Two things you do not typically like, let alone allow: water play and fighting.

You're doing it!

Absolutely do not add to the chaos, you think.

The scene has become noisy in all ways and you do your best to stay calm. It isn't going to be perfect, but you're making a valiant effort.

"I will join you when I am done. In about twenty minutes."

This isn't the easy or even comfortable solution, but it is the right one in this moment.

You are committed to changing the dynamics at home, and you know that the journey toward change is never smooth; it is always easier to take the well-worn path. You're going to have to fight through the bramble. But you can do it. Even when it feels pokey and unfamiliar and scary.

Before they retreat from you, you remind them to close the door behind them.

You readjust the shower temperature up a bit. You will keep your promise to your family members and will connect with them in twenty minutes, but, until that time, you must focus on yourself. As you lean your hair back into the stream of hot water washing away the stress of the muddy moment, you can't help but laugh.

By giving yourself this small window of time, you are not only providing clear boundaries to your family members, but you're giving your teen a real-life example of stellar behavior modeling. Every person should be able to carve out a little space in their day during which time they can do/listen to/feel/say/or turn-the-water-temperature-up-to whatever they want.

You're going to be responsible for so much heavy-duty parenting in the days, weeks, months, years to come; modeling behavior is a way for you to show them something important without it being a tense or teaching moment. Also, you need to be clean.

You turn your focus back to all things soapy. You decide this is the perfect time to use the special body scrub you splurged on recently but have not yet had the chance to use. As you massage the pink gel into your skin, you exfoliate any traces of guilt. You spend a whole ten minutes in the shower, towel off, take time to use a serum on your face, a moisturizer on your body, and a leave-in treatment in your hair before wrapping it into a drying towel. You have five minutes before you'll be expected outside, and you consider leaving the bathroom early, but you remind yourself how important these clear boundaries are for *everyone*

Consistency is key.

This is the bramble.

The yucky thoughts continue to try to worm their way into your mind, but you keep reminding yourself that you've raised a good kid, that they will be okay, and that nothing about their life or friendships or future will be decided in the span of this shower. Right now, they are busy with a very dirty dog and that is exactly how it should be.

You stay on the path. You stand in front of the mirror in the steamy room and floss your teeth. Something just for you.

After exactly twenty minutes you head out, get dressed, and meet your wet, giggling family members outside.

"You came!" your teen says, sounding like a much younger child. You're showing them that people can be trusted. This is such a good, important thing. This is connection.

"Of course, I did. I keep my promises."

Everything about you—from your skin to your conscience—feels clean and fresh, and you know you've done the thing. The harder, brambly thing. And you'll keep on going, and make a new well-worn path, and you will all be better for it.

You always are.

Congratulations! You've Collected Coping Mechanism Badge of *Connection Cornerstone*.

Turn to page 152 to return to the story.

CHOICE 2: You accept the chaos.

You take a beat, as your instinct to hop out and help surfaces. That's just what you do.

Instead of delaying the inevitable, you flip the valve so water goes from the shower head to the bathtub spout, grab a towel, and step out of the shower carefully. And seething. Seethingly careful.

Or, carefully seething.

Your teen and partner work together to hoist Crosby into the tub and you take your post at his back half, holding him still.

At that moment, your other child, the younger tween, bursts into the bathroom and, seemingly oblivious to the chore, starts asking, on repeat, "Can I order the merch from the most famous YouTuber ever?? Please? Can I? Pretty please?"

"Sweetie," you remain calm, using every ounce of willpower you can muster.

"Right now, I cannot focus on merch or YouTube or whatever merch a YouTuber could possibly be selling. Do you not see what's happening right now?"

"Fine!" your tween pouts, as though they are the only one suffering.

Your teen turns on the sprayer, aims it at Crosby, who is, indeed, covered in something brown, and turns it on.

And then, things devolve into pure chaos.

You look down at your precious little dog and, for one instant, but before you can react, you know exactly what is about to happen.

"NOOOOOOOOOOOOO!" echoes through the small bathroom, but your cry is in vain, as the dog shakes himself vigorously, back and forth, soaking you, your partner, and your teen in brown water.

"Why couldn't you just handle things?" you continue your shouting. "I handle things all day, every day, and I just needed a shower, because I hadn't showered in two days, and I am sick of being busy and tired and dirty and alone in all of it!"

Your yell seems to reverberate endlessly. Your insides match your outsides, all messy and mucky and grimy feeling. You've raised your voice. You hate raising your voice. It was one of the things you'd sworn you'd never do in those glowy, pre-parenthood days. And you'd stuck to it! Most of the time . . .

This time, you lost control. And so, you commit to taking it back.

In order to assuage your guilt, you have to take the opposite action, as you'd learned years ago, and apologize. You know that apologizing is something that can be hard, uncomfortable, and, at the same time, vital to model for your kids. We all make mistakes, mess up, say, or do or feel something that belies our character.

The important thing is the repair.

The reconnection.

The resilience.

In order to practice the *opposite action* technique, you make sure to pause and reflect, in order to be as thoughtful and intentional as possible.

You feel guilty, yes, but is that guilt justified? In this situation, the content of what you were saying was fair and true, but you should not have yelled. That is clear. The only way to take back the power in this situation, and to alleviate these burdensome feelings of guilt, is to do the opposite action to what you'd done before. Before, you yelled. Now, you will apologize.

You know that any opposite action feels uncomfortable and that you'll have to tolerate feeling unsettled for a bit. And you remind yourself that it will pass.

"I am so sorry. I didn't mean to yell. I should not have yelled, and I tried my best to stay calm. I am feeling overwhelmed, and this is how it came out. Please accept my apology."

You are proud of yourself, as you were honest, clear, and, most of all, showed grace. You've modeled a crucial interpersonal skill for your teen, and you know that it will pay off in all of their relationships—with teachers, with parents, and, you are confident, with peers.

Inspired by your grace, your partner speaks. "I am sorry too. You deserved this peace and quiet. I shouldn't have left the kids alone."

You feel seen. You feel grateful. You feel . . .

Wet.

Crosby, still wet and muddy in the tub, shook his body once more, spraying you with the gross, brown water.

You look up at your teen, expecting to see disappointment in their giant eyes, but you're surprised to see them doubled over in hysterical, body-quaking laughter—contagious, beautiful laughter. As you sit together on the bathroom floor, just two parents, their kid, a wet dog, and brown water, you laugh until your bellies hurt.

"Can I help you to clean up?" your child asks, hopefully.

"Who are you and what did you do with my teenager?"

"I feel bad. I'll help."

Together, you slowly, methodically, take on the challenge. You're working so well together, more connected than you've been in a long time.

A little vulnerability can go a long way.

As they finish toweling off Crosby's kinky hair, your partner stands and beckons for your child.

"Come on. Time to take him outside. You have an extremely dirty parent who needs not to be."

You all laugh and settle into the next stage of the evening together, as a team.

You are reminded of something you'd not understood when your kids were little, and everything was measured in Facebook albums and status updates: that *special time* doesn't have to mean taking your kids to a sporting event or visiting a museum or creating an elaborate scavenger hunt in the backyard. Your kids, like all kids, really just yearn for *engaged time* when they have your undivided attention—when you can do nothing together and nothing becomes everything.

"Sorry, again, love," you say, as they head out the bathroom door.

They smile back at you. All feels okay. Not great, but okay.

If your teen can forgive you, you realize that you can, and should, forgive *yourself*.

And that's what you do.

Congratulations! You've Collected Coping Mechanism Badge of *Transformation Triumph*.

Turn to page 152 to return to the story.

BONUS: Create a More/Less Inventory

Using your remarkable insight and bolstered flexibility, create two lists that show what you need from your family members. Keep in mind that these lists can, and should, grow and evolve. On the first list, name everything that you need more of. On the second list, name the things you need to have and do and feel less. In the spirit of connectedness, ask your family members to do the same. Share your lists with one another if it feels appropriate. Do with them what you wish. Use this as a chance to take a personal inventory of what you're getting, needing, wanting, and feeling from your current family dynamics. Once you know where you want to be, you can make a plan to get there.

I Need More of . . .

I Need Less of . . .

Dear Person or People Who Love a Parent,

Let me start out by saying how awesome it is that you are here. Just the fact that you've decided to show up—that you are validating the parent's feelings and showing the parent support means so much and makes a difference!

Studies have shown that the act of connection between parents and their peers (whether family members, friends, or acquaintances) can improve mental health outcomes by statistically significant amounts. So, you're off to a great start.

Within these pages you will read stories of parents who may or may not seem like the parents you know, as some of the details will be different, but I can guarantee you that many of the parents you know are harder on themselves than they need to be. How can you help? That's such a great question, I'm happy to tell you.

First, by just showing up. You've already done that. You're ahead of the game. Truthfully, the feeling of loneliness, whether or not someone is actually alone, can be so damaging to the psyche making the tough stuff even tougher. Support is crucial to success.

Second, don't judge. I know this goes without saying and I know it is not in your nature to judge, and I know that when you do, rarely, make a judgement it is done with only the best of intentions and out of the goodness of your heart. But I can assure you that your judgment, is not necessary nor appreciated nor appropriate. The parent you are tempted to judge is already judging themself enough. Just for the sake of clarity, please see the following scientific chart.

As you can see, there is never a time in which it is appropriate to judge a parent who is trying their very best.

Times when you are allowed to judge a parent who is doing their best:

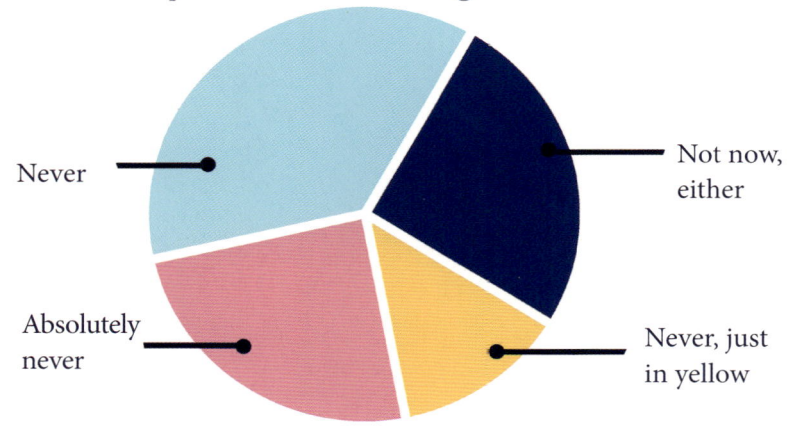

- Never
- Absolutely never
- Never, just in yellow
- Not now, either

Third, take the time to give parents you know some regular, specific compliments. "You're doing a great job" is easy to tune out, especially when a person is in distress. Instead, offer notes on things you've observed, for example: "You did a great job handling that conflict this morning and staying so calm" or "That's awesome that you cooked dinner for your kid."

Be a flattering mirror in which the parents you love can view themselves. Sometimes, that's all that takes. Now, head on back to page 11 and enjoy this book as a sympathetic supporter. While you might not relate to all of the details of the stories, there are tips and strategies that can be used by anyone. Thank you for your allyship and support. Parenthood is most definitely a team sport, and so thank you for wearing our pinny.

With love,

a parent who someone knows

155

Badge Index and Celebratory Sash Ceremony

Congratulations! Welcome to your Sash Ceremony!

You've done it!!! You've made it through all of the hard things, one step, one test, one small triumph at a time.

Along the way, you've collected many badges, and now it is time to receive your sash.

Oh my goodness, it looks amazing on you!

The master list of all of your badges, as well as descriptions of each coping skill it signifies, can be found below. While you haven't historically been a sash person, this accessory is simply a reminder of all you can do and all you can be. In short, you've rocked this.

Let your badges remind you that life is messy, things happen, and challenges arise, but you know that you can handle every obstacle that is thrown your way.

It won't always feel great, but you'll always do great. Even if it takes a couple of tries. Using these coping mechanisms, you can do your best to avoid the guilt or, when you can't avoid it, sidestep it. Now you have the tools to assuage these feelings when they do arise.

Whether it's a new skill from the practices of CBT or DBT, an activity that serves to distract or delight you, or simply a new way of breathing, you're now ready to take on the world. One texture-sensitive LEGO pirate at a time.

Okay, mom. Time to step out in that sash and wear it with pride! Or, if you prefer, put it in a special place for you to return to any time you need the reminder. Either way, this is yours, and nothing can change that. No misstep will ever dim the light you shine upon yourself and your family. This sash is non-returnable, non-transferable, and never goes out of style. Embrace it, own it, and never forget the incredible journey you've traveled. Here's to you, mom, and all the adventures still waiting to unfold. You're unstoppable.

Index of Badges

Below is the list of exciting, important coping mechanism badges you've earned along your journey. Though they have whimsical names or playful hooks, each one is grounded in evidence-based practice aimed at enriching your well-being and bolstering your resilience.

Sensory Grounding:

Sensory Grounding: Learning to focus on the senses to anchor oneself in the present moment and reduce emotional distress.

Square Breathing:

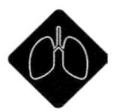

Square Breathing: A relaxation technique involving inhaling, holding, exhaling, and pausing for equal intervals to promote calmness and reduce stress.

Boundaries Boss:

Boundary Building: Establishing and maintaining clear personal boundaries to protect your emotional well-being and integrity in relationships.

Persistent Protector:

Broken Record Technique: Repeatedly asserting one's boundaries or needs calmly and assertively in the face of resistance or pressure.

Outstanding Observer:

Observe and Describe: Noticing and objectively describing thoughts, feelings, and sensations without judgment or interpretation.

Mindful Mapper:

Body Scan Exercise: A mindfulness practice involving systematically focusing attention on different parts of the body to promote relaxation and self-awareness.

Pep-Talk Prodigy:

Self-Encouragement Message: Writing and referring to a supportive and encouraging note to yourself to boost confidence and motivation.

Dialectical Dynamo:

Employing Dialectical Thinking: Embracing the idea that opposing viewpoints or experiences can coexist and balancing between the differing viewpoints and experiences.

Tranquil Traveler:

Mindful Driving: Applying mindfulness principles, such as staying present and focused, while driving to enhance safety and reduce stress.

Acceptance Ally:

Non-Judgmental Stance: Adopting an attitude of acceptance and openness towards oneself and others without harsh criticism or evaluation.

Flow Facilitator:

Cognitive Diffusion: Detaching from unhelpful thoughts by viewing them as passing mental events rather than factual truths.

Distress Dossier:

Activity Record: Keeping track of things and activities that help you in times of distress, to have on hand when you need them.

F.A.S.T. Friend:

F.A.S.T. Skill: A DBT skill for applying Fair, No Apologies, Stick to Values, and Truthful principles to maintain self-respect and boundaries in relationships.

G.I.V.E. Guru:

G.I.V.E. Skill: A DBT skill for using Gentle, Interested, Validate, and Easy manner to effectively communicate and resolve interpersonal conflicts.

Heart & Head Harmony:

Wise Mind: A DBT skill used for integrating both emotional and logical aspects of decision-making and problem-solving to achieve balanced and effective outcomes.

S.T.O.P. Star:

Interpersonal Communication S.T.O.P. Skill: A DBT skill for pausing in communication to Self-soothe, Take a step back, Observe, and Proceed mindfully to improve interpersonal interactions.

Connection Cornerstone:

Nurtured Heart Approach: Cultivating an environment of positivity and recognition to foster emotional growth and resilience.

Transformation Triumph:

Opposite Action: A DBT skill focused on acting in a manner contrary to one's emotional urges to reduce the intensity of negative emotions and promote positive change.

Notes

Marsha M. Linehan, *DBT (R) Skills Training Handouts and Worksheets* 2nd ed (New York, NY: Guilford Publications, 2014).

Michael Rosen, *We're Going on a Bear Hunt* (London, England: Walker Books, 2016).

Marsha M. Linehan, *DBT (R) Skills Training Handouts and Worksheets* 2nd ed (New York, NY: Guilford Publications, 2014).

Further Reading

Acceptance and Commitment Therapy: The Process and Practice of Mindful Change by S.C. Hayes, K.D. Strosahl, & K.G. Wilson

DBT Skills Training Handouts and Worksheets, 2nd edition by Marsha M. Linehan

Transforming the Difficult Child: The Nurtured Heart Approach by Howard Glasser and Jennifer Easley

About Familius

Visit Our Website: www.familius.com

Familius is a global trade publishing company that publishes books and other content to help families be happy. We believe that happy families are key to a better society and the foundation of a happy life. The greatest work anyone will ever do will be within the walls of his or her own home. And we don't mean vacuuming! We recognize that every family looks different and passionately believe in helping all families find greater joy, whatever their situation. To that end, we publish beautiful books that help families live our 10 Habits of Happy Family Life: *love together, play together, learn together, work together, talk together, heal together, read together, eat together, give together,* and *laugh together*. Further, Familius does not discriminate on the basis of race, color, religion, gender, age, nationality, disability, caste, or sexual orientation in any of its activities or operations. Founded in 2012, Familius is located in Sanger, California.

Connect

Facebook: www.facebook.com/familiusbooks
Pinterest: www.pinterest.com/familiusbooks
Instagram: @FamiliusBooks
TikTok: @FamiliusBooks

The most important work you ever do will be within the walls of your own home.

About the Author

Rebecca Fox Starr, LMSW, is a mom, author, mental health professional, dedicated to normalizing mental health issues for all.

Rebecca has authored three books on the subject: "Beyond the Baby Blues" (Rowman & Littlefield, January 2018), "Baby Ever After" (Rowman & Littlefield, available January 31, 2021), and "Mommy Ever After" (Familius, 2022), and "Am I doing This Right (Familius, 2025). She has also advocated all across the country for equity in maternal mental healthcare.

She works as a clinical therapist and lives outside of Philadelphia with her husband, two kids, and two scruffy dogs.

6